AF654881

Students in the Field: An Experimental Learning

About the Author

Prof. Ganapathy Palanithurai, Rajiv Gandhi Chair for Panchayati Raj Studies, Department of Political Science and Development Administration, Gandhigram Rural Institute – Deemed University, Gandhigram is an academic activist working with academic community, civil society, policy community and political community to impress upon them the importance and need of democratic local governance in India to enable the poor to lead a decent dignified human life. All his academic, research and outreach activities are being supported by an array of funding agencies namely the World Bank, the UNDP, the UNICEF, the Hunger Project, SDC, DANIDA, Action Aid International, the Ford Foundation, Population Foundation of India, the Rajiv Gandhi Foundation, Toolkit Foundation Netherland, Ministry of Panchayati Raj and State Planning Commission. He was a Visiting Professor in Cologne University, Germany. He has to his credit seventy-three books, 126 research articles, 112 popular articles in popular newspapers, 83 monographs published in a span of three decades. He is the coordinator of UGC-SAP and UGC innovative programme. He held several administrative positions like Dean, Faculty of Social Sciences, Dean Student's Welfare, Member, Syndicate, Member Senate, Member, and Academic Council in Gandhigram Rural Institute. He was and is member of many advisory committees of the Government of India and Government of Tamil Nadu pertinent to local governance and rural development.

Students in the Field

An Experimental Learning

(Village Placement Programme)

G. Palanithurai

CONCEPT PUBLISHING COMPANY PVT. LTD.
NEW DELHI-110059

© Author

All rights reserved. No part of this work may be reproduced, stored, adapted, or transmitted in any form or by any means, electronic, mechanical, photocopying, micro-filming recording or otherwise, or translated in any language, without the prior written permission of the copyright owner and the publisher. The book is sold subject to the condition that it shall not, by way of trade or otherwise, be lent, resold, hired out, or otherwise circulated without the prior publisher's written consent in any form of binding or cover other than that in which it is published.

The views and opinions expressed in this book are author(s) own and the facts reported by them/her have been verified to the extent possible, and the publishers are not in any way liable for the same.

ISBN-13: 978-93-5125-141-5

First Published 2015

Published and Printed by

Concept
Since 1974

Concept Publishing Company Pvt. Ltd.
A/15-16, Commercial Block, Mohan Garden
New Delhi-110059 (India)
T: 25351460, 25351794, *F*: 091-11-25357109
E: publishing@conceptpub.com, W: www.conceptpub.com
Editorial Office: H-13, Bali Nagar. New Delhi-110 015, India.

Cataloging in Publication Data—*Courtesy:* D.K. Agencies (P) Ltd. <docinfo@dkagencies.com>

Palanithurai, G., author.
Students in the field : an experimental learning (Village Placement Programme) / G. Palanithurai.
pages cm
ISBN 9789351251415

1. Gandhigram Rural Institute. Village Placement Programme. 2. Fieldwork (Educational method)--India--Tamil Nadu. 3. Rural development--India--Palayamkottai--Fieldwork. I. Title.

DDC 373.095482 23

To

Divine Mother

Preface

In Gandhigram Rural Institute, a centrally funded Deemed University has an extension programme which has been termed as Village Placement Programme. Under this programme students have to be placed in a village for a week. It is mandatory for every student. Hence, in the Department of Political Science and Development Administration annually students of M.A Development Administration and M.A Governance and Development are placed in a village setting for a full week for their learning through staying and working with people in the rural areas. This Programme is common one for all the degree programmes. It is unique to the Gandhigram Rural Institute. Each and every Department has to carry out this Programme. As a result one could see the impact in the students coming out from this institute. Impact could be seen in the students in the form of a skill in working with communities and more specifically the rustic folk. Essentially it is designed to train, orient and sensitize the students in rural socio-economic realities. Hands on experience in development practice will enable the students to gain deeper understanding into the social and economic transformative process of the rustic folk. Staying with community will bridge the gap between the book view and field reality. It is always designed in such a way that the difficult realities of the rural setting could be realized by the students in staying in the rural settings in difficult conditions. Since, it is a learning programme, it has to be designed, executed and evaluated only by effective participation of the students. It is not a Programme designed by the teachers and carried out by the students. Essentially it should be a Programme of the students facilitated by the teachers. Role of the teacher is vital but very limited and the space for students is huge. In the whole process of designing and executing the entire programme has to be done by the students. At every stage the teachers have to facilitate the students. Students should find passion in working in the programme. Then only they give their soul and spirit in the programme. The evaluation has to be done by the teachers who are in charge of the programme. It is an annual programme. Every year they have to be placed in the field for a week. Teachers will be with them and enable them to do all the activities. The cost of their stay will be shared by the students and the institute.

This year I took responsibility of going with the students to Village Placement Programme. I have decided to put the students in a Dalit village so that they can understand their problems more and they will be sensitized on the issues of the marginalised. Against the backdrop the programme was designed and it was proposed to be conducted in Palayamkottai Gram Panchayat in Aathur Block of Dindigul district, Tamil Nadu.

In the seven days stay of the students in the village, the activities carried out by the students have been documented. The documentation was also done by the students. The students' documents have been converted into a monograph form by me as a coordinator and the same is presented for the benefits of the students and teachers of other universities and colleges. This monograph will give ideas about how beneficially field placements can be arranged for master students in universities. Essentially it deals with the experiential learning of the students when they are placed in the villages. It is a learning not only for the students but also for the teachers. This programme will be a powerful tool of teaching and learning for both the students and the teachers. Activities were designed for our student's course requirements and our understanding. It can be modified to suit the requirements of other subject students. Of course, in many institutions field works are being carried but they are not properly documented. This kind of programme can be organised by any higher learning institutions for any group of students pursuing any programme be it a medical college or a law college or an arts and science college or agriculture college.

G. Palanithurai

Acknowledgements

No work can be done individually in the world. I strongly feel that all the works either in the job or in family or in the community are the outcome of the efforts of many. The Village Placement Programme (VPP) is the outcome of the efforts of many though major activities are designed and carried out by the students. Students of the two programmes have been classified into two groups. First group was placed in a Dalit village in a community hall. The second group was placed in another Dalit village at Kadavur Village Panchayat. For the two programmes my colleagues extended their support by coming to the field and work with the students.

I have to mention more specifically Dr. Ranjith Kumar, newly appointed Assistant Professor in the Department of Political Science and Development Administration. He did his M.A. in our Department and Ph.D in Pondicherry University. He knew thoroughly about the Village Placement Programme as he underwent the same programme when he was a master student in our university. Hence, it was easy for me to make the students to design the programme. Equally my JRF Ph.D scholar Ms. K. Aruna who stayed with girl students for full seven days in the village. There are other scholars namely Mr. P. Sathyaraj, Mr. D. Sivakumar, Mr. G. George, Mr. Jayarajan and Mr. B.E. George Dimtrov and a few others who worked tirelessly to make the programme a very useful and successful one. I express my thanks to those who involved in the programme. I further extend my warmest thanks to my students for their commitment and sincerity while they were on the job in the village.

Further I express my deep sense of gratitude to the people who are living nearer to the building where our students stayed as they took special care of my students. During the scarcity of water our students were allowed to use their personal toilets and bathrooms. There are a few youth, men and women, who were with our students when they were conducting surveys in the village. Apart from the above, there were two Block Development Officers who came to the camp and briefed about the role of Panchayati Raj in the rural development process to the students. A catering team assisted our students by preparing food for the students at an affordable cost. During the programme Panchayat ward members have helped our students to make use of the Panchayat office and furniture and other facilities. For all those who helped our students to conduct activities in the villages in Village Placement Programme, I register my sincere thanks. In yet another camp, former Vice-Chancellor Dr. N. Markandan came and reviewed the activities of the students. I express my sense of gratitude to him. Finally, I register my thanks to my family unit wife Smt. Mala.

G. Palanithurai

Contents

List of Tables

List of Boxes

1
Introduction

It is an axiomatic truth that there is a close relationship between the level of education and the level of development in a society. But the way in which the educational system is designed and run, accordingly it will yield results. Primarily knowledge and skill will play a predominant role in transforming the society. Higher learning institutions are the key instruments to produce knowledge and create skills. It does not mean people do not have knowledge and skills. They have knowledge and skills but they are being shaped to the requirement of the society to enhance the living standard of the people. So knowledge production, knowledge updation and knowledge dissemination have to be done by higher learning institutions. Equally the skills have to be created, updated and sharpened to the requirements level by the higher level institutions. The above activities have to be done by the higher learning institutions through three ways. They are through research, academic and outreach programmes. In India, it is very rare to find all the three essential functions in higher learning institutions. Many institutions have only academic programmes and they run graduate and post-graduate programmes along with research leading to Ph.D degree. There are institutions which run both academic programmes from certificate course to Ph.D degree along with large number of research activities. The research activities are of both pure and action oriented. These types of institutions are not large in number in India. Of course, there are pure research institutions without having academic programmes.

Apart from the above there are academic institutions which are performing all the three dimensional activities namely, research, academic and outreach by giving equal importance to all the three dimensions. Giving justice to all the three dimensions in terms of activities in the higher learning institutions is not so easy in Indian context. In India, it is only the Agriculture Universities performing all the three functions. In the course of years even the agriculture universities could not do justice to extension activities and as a result Krishi Vigyan Kendras were established throughout the country.

Apart from the above, the Gandhigram Rural Institute is the only institute performing all the three dimensional activities as it was established only for outreach activities and now it became a full-fledged centrally funded deemed university. Carrying out all the three dimensional activities pose tremendous challenges to the quantity and quality output and outcome of the institute. Yet it continues to perform the three dimensional activities. For academic and research activities, there have been well laid norms, evaluative tools and mechanisms are in place. For extension we are guiding ourselves as we are the pioneers as our institute was established at the dawn of independence. The outreach programme designed in the initial formative years of the institute was service oriented. Providing services to poor, farmers, and women and marginalized were the core activities of the institute. But that have not been continued as Government slowly established its departments and delivered variety of services to the people. Later instead of service they started providing ideas, knowledge, skill, technology, institutional framework, and consultancy to the society directly through outreach programmes. But these activities have been continuously undergone changes. As the Gandhigram Rural Institute emerged as a full-fledged deemed university having 3500 students including research scholars through its academic programmes along with heavily funded projects, designing and operating an outreach programme for the benefit of both communities and students is the difficult exercise. There are many outreach programmes being carried out from the action projects, and from the academic programmes in our institute. Designing outreach programme for three thousand five hundred students is not an easy task. Students should have scientific rural exposure and they should have take away from the outreach programme for their learning and at the same time the rural community should not feel that their normal life is being disturbed because of the outreach programme designed and carried out in the villages. In such a way the outreach programme is to be designed with great difficulty and carried out in the rural areas for the past several decades.

Moreover, it has to provide opportunity for the teachers to have take away from the outreach programme. There are many outreach programmes embedded in the curriculum. They are academic programme based, course based, research based, project based and institute based and they are being carried out in different nomenclatures. They are: extension education, extension work, field work, weekly field visits, internship, placement, and night stay, programme visit and so on. Every work has its own implication in the learning process of the programme. This village placement programme is designed for all the students of all the programmes in our institute. It is mandatory that every student has to undergo seven days full stay in the villages in an academic year. It will be done in an odd semester. A three year programme student will stay two times in the village placement programme. It is a mandatory activity for every student in this university. This programme is apart from other extension activities of specific degree programmes. It has its own evaluation and assessment. The rigour and intensity of the programme depends on the teachers, students and the department. But there are overall guidance for the programme and programme evaluation. There are departments which carry out the programme very intensively, creatively and passionately with the satisfaction of the students and the community in the rural areas. It could be seen in the overall total evaluation of the programmes conducted by the university. Seriousness of the programme could be seen in the overall programme context. It implies that the seriousness of the village placement programme could be seen in the overall context of the academic programme and the personality of the institute. Yet rigour could be seen while the teacher concerned takes serious efforts. Hence, it is totally in the hands of the teachers who coordinate the programme. Because he is always with the students. If a department is serious in offering the entire academic programme, one will expect the same seriousness in the Village Placement Programme (VPP) also. Further seriousness depends on the teacher who offers courses and coordinates Village Placement

Programme. If the teacher who coordinate with interest and passion with full understanding of the importance and implications of the programme, the teacher will create such consciousness among the students. Thus students will also come to the expected level of the teacher. As a result the whole programme will be carried out in a joyful mode. Students and teachers will do the programme seriously and get huge take away from the programme for the students and the teachers. Primarily energy has to come from the teachers for the programme. Logistic problems they face will not be a hindrance to the learning process in the programme. Higher the logistic problems higher will be the learning possibilities. Staying in a village where they face water scarcity will not pose a problem to the students if they are oriented to study the coping up mechanisms the community has developed over a period of time to face water scarcity. Higher the problems in the villages, higher the possibilities for the students to learn and work. Normally in a conventional sense teachers use to prefer the villages which are having more facilities for the stay of the students to minimize the hardship of the teachers and students. Difficult physical conditions will enable the students to learn more about deprivation and its implications.

An experienced teacher will always prefer to go to a village where more problems persist. Because students will get more exposure on the problems faced by the people who are living in the rural areas. Apart from the exposure, the students will be sensitized on the issues faced by the rustic folk. I always choose the different situation for the students in the villages where they stay. No doubt the teachers have more problems and risks. The teacher who is coordinating the village placement programme has to orient the students in such a way that they should feel that they have lot of opportunities for learning. To place the students in the village, we need to have the consent of the local communities and Panchayats because we need to use the official machinery for the programme. If we want to use the community hall for our students stay we need to get permission from the Panchayat. When we want to use the common toilets for girls which are being used by Self-Help-Groups, we need to get permission from SHG leaders and Panchayats. likewise to use the Panchayat office and office furniture, we need permission again from Panchayats. Hence, before finalizing the programme the coordinator and a few students have to visit the village and establish rapport with community and the Panchayat Institution. As we explain to the students about the Village Placement Programme, we have to brief the members of the community and Panchayat functionaries about the programme clearly. In any account we should not give any room for expectation to be generated from the people or from the Panchayats. It is to be informed that it is only for the purpose of learning for the students and the people and not for any other purpose. In the same way people should not be disturbed. If the students stay in the school, on any account the classes should not be affected. Village placement programme should not be at the cost of the villagers. By keeping the above aspects in the backdrop, the activities have to be decided and designed. Based on the students' curiosity and relevance to the subjects, activities have to be designed. Once activities are designed how the activities are to be carried have to do be fixed. Well designed activities will bring lot of learning to the students and execution will not be a problem at all. As our students are pursuing development administration focus should be more on the issues of development, governance, politics and administration. Of course, cross cutting issues will also be focused. Culture, gender, marginalization, and exclusion will find focus in the programme. Each village has its own unique practices and features and they are to be focused. In the backdrop of the above we have decided to place our students in a Dalit dominated village Palayamkottai Village Panchayat in Aathur Block of Dindigul district. Here, it is to be noted that there is no direction or guidelines from the UGC for extension activities to be done by the higher learning institutions. In the UGC framework of activities of higher learning institutions, there are guidelines for academic programmes and research activities but there is no guideline for extension activities. Yet Gandhigram Rural Institute gives equal importance to extension programmes.

2
A Framework for Village Placement Programme

1. Why this Stay in Villages?

The reasons are:

- to offer an opportunity to the students to understand the different facets of the rural community; to enable the students to relate and comprehend classroom learning to field realities; to facilitate the students to evolve methodological nuances to interact with rustic folk and work with them; to share information related to governance, administration and development with the people; to facilitate the students to understand the process of development and rural transformation; to facilitate the initiation and sustenance of socially relevant programmes/projects that will benefit the rural community; to facilitate the students to evolve researchable problems; to inculcate socially relevant values and responsibilities among the students; to make the students to understand the process of social and economic transformation, and to enable the students to understand the differences and disparities among the collectivities in the villages.

2. Types of Activities

When the students are in the villages, people in the village should feel that they are getting some benefits out of it. They should not feel that they are deprived of something. In such a way, the camp has to be designed and organised. Students should connect themselves with community consciously. Village placement programmes should not be converted into exclusive manual labour camps. Camps must be lively and should bubble with interesting activities. The students and staff must enjoy every minute of their stay. The villagers must also enjoy "our presence" in the village. Hence, it is essential to have a judicious mix of different activities. A tentative list of activities and time allotted for each activity are suggested below:

Types of activity	*No. of hours per day*
Manual labour – may be used as a rapport building exercise; may be employed to create assets (to understand the value of manual labour) More efforts have to be taken to involve villagers also	2 (It can be increased or decreased based on the need)
Interaction – with different sections of people through participatory methods (it should be meaningful and win win for both)	3 (Interaction based on well defined discourse topics)
Visit – to local level institutions—formal and informal (without disturbing their regular activities)	1 (Visits should enable the students to bring data, facts or ideas for discussion)
Competition and Contests – among the students on a chosen theme – may be an essay or a debating competition	1 (Competition should be on the works and activities of the camp)
Dialogue – with the students and the members of staff (recapitulation, reviews and clarifications with reference to theory)	2 (Meaningful reviews should enable them to move to higher level of understanding)
Lecture – on rural oriented subjects	1 (Experts relevant to the camp)
Report writing and evaluation	1 (Students have to learn the art of report writing)
Socio-Cultural activities	1 (It should be on a relevant theme useful to the community)
Total	**12**

This chapter is not written for our students alone. It was prepared by the institute for all the students of university. I have only a few things to suit our need.

They are suggestive and basic. Innovatively and creatively programme can be designed and carried out. The activities suggested need not be considered as a blueprint. Only broad guidelines are given. The staff, after assessing the local situation and condition and by using their ingenuity, can chalk out a village-specific programme. The programme should be flexible and adaptable. However, a session on report writing and evaluation should be incorporated as an essential component in the schedule of activities. It is to be noted that the whole programme should be designed through a participatory process. Students should be the main stakeholders and they should be in charge of designing the programme and the teachers have to facilitate them.

3. Department of Extension Education (in Gandhigram Rural Institute we have a Department for Extension Education)

Role and Responsibilities

The Department of Extension Education will serve as facilitation unit. It will perform the following duties: (a) Help individual departments in selecting villages; (b) Arrange review meetings if necessary; (c) Help in documenting the placement experiences; (d) Coordinate the placement activities of different departments; (e) Assist in evaluation wherever possible and needed; (f) Enabling the departments to face constraints in organizing the VPP.

4. Tips to Organize the VPP

(a) Pre-camp arrangements (For Teachers)

- Make a visit to a few villages keeping the requirement in the backdrop.
- Make two or three visits to the village (mostly in the evenings) where the camp is going to be organized. Take two or three students with you.

- Meet the Gram Panchayat Elected Representatives.
- Meet different kinds of people, leaders of different kind and establish rapport with them.
- Explain to them the purpose and objectives of the proposed camp.
- See that adequate toilet facilities available in the village Panchayat.
- Design manual labour projects after consulting the Panchayat representatives.
- Take only such items of work which could be completed within the seven days.
- Discuss and decide the place of stay – a separate place for women with toilet facilities.
- Meet the students once or twice prior to the camp and orient them on the camp.
- Prepare a day-wise schedule of activities; let it be flexible and adaptable.
- Distribute the programme schedule to the students in advance.
- Make necessary arrangements to cook food for the campers like buying provisions, hiring cooking vessels, cook, etc. Let the food be simple vegetarian and nutritious.
- Local products have to be purchased.
- Prepare menu for the camp period in consultation with the students.
- Instruct the students to come with simple bedding, a tumbler and a plate, a note book, a few white sheets and a pen.
- Let the students be divided into small groups depending on the number of students. Let there be a leader for each group.
- Let each and every activity designed to be managed by the students and their leaders. Let the staff members be just facilitators.
- Training materials have to be provided in the camp.

(b) During the camp (For Teachers)

- Strict adherence to time schedule.
- See that all campers stay in one place.

- Make the camp lively, meaningful and enjoyable.
- Enforce strict discipline.
- Ensure the safety of the students at all times.
- Schedule a time for writing field notes everyday. At least an hour should be allotted for the purpose.
- Cultural programmes organized by the students should be seen before they are being conducted.
- Let the students and staffs meet to discuss how the day's programme was carried out and how the next day's programme should be carried out.
- Ensure that there is perfect cooperation and coordination among the students.
- Ensure people's participation in all the activities as far as possible.
- Visit the places wherever students are in action.
- See that the accounts related to the camp are written everyday.
- Transparency has to be maintained.
- Ensure that all equipments/implements are to be returned to the units wherefrom they have taken.
- Take attendance in the morning and also in the night before the campers go to bed
- On the final day, ensure the following:
  - Meet the people and thank them
  - Return back the materials taken from the local people
  - Return back the materials taken from the Panchayat office
  - Write a report on the activities during the camp
  - Evaluation of the camp
  - Convene a meeting of the students and appreciate them for their cooperation in conducting the camp
  - Cleaning the place of stay and kitchen
  - Taking stock of unused provisions and implements
  - A formal letter of thanks to be submitted to the Panchayat.

(c) *After the camp*

- Settle the advance immediately

- Send copies of the camp report to:
  - ➢ Departments of extension education for consolidation; and
  - ➢ GRI news for publication.
- Arrange for a review meeting at the department level
- Decide the follow-up activities, if any.

5. Feedback

It is always necessary to have the feedback on the placement programme. The feedback programme will help us to understand the feelings and opinion of the students. It will enable us to ascertain where we could have done better. Hence, it is essential to integrate evaluation component in our extension programme. A suggestive list of questions is presented below. You may have to add your own.

- What are the various components of extension work carried out in the village?
- What are the components which you like the most?
- What are the components which you like the least?
- Are you able to relate your learning in class room with field realities? Specify.
- What lessions have you learnt from the Village Placement Programme?
- Specify the problems, if any, you have faced during the placement
- How can a placement of this type be arranged better next time?

6. Do's and Don't's (For the Students)

Do's	*Dont's*
✓ Be interested in learning from the people	× Don't lecture
	× Don't dominate
✓ Mix with the community members	× Don't rush
	× Don't loiter

(*Contd.*)

(*Contd.*)

Do's	*Dont's*
✓ Respect the community members and their knowledge ✓ Respect local customs ✓ Be punctual ✓ Be open-minded ✓ Be sincere ✓ Be regular ✓ Be attentive ✓ Be sensitive to local issues ✓ Be self-critical ✓ Be humble ✓ Work in groups ✓ Develop the tendency to conceptualize what you have seen, observed and learnt ✓ Schedule timing for writing field report	× Don't assume × Don't concentrate on only one segment of the population × Don't leave the camp without the knowledge of the teacher × Don't smoke × Don't take bath in open wells and streams, if you don't know swimming × Don't use costly eateries × Don't prepare rich food in the villages

7. Basics of Village Development

(For Information to Students)

1. **What is village society?**
   - Understanding the village culture, economy, structure, customs, livelihood, governance, administration, social relationship, institutional arrangements and organizational set-up.
2. **What is Development?**
   - The process has to be studied.
3. **What is responsible well-being?**
   - Responsible well-being means attainments of quality of life

- Make the difference between quality of life and standard of life.

4. **What factors determine responsible well-being?**
   - Human Development, well-being, human dignity and factors affecting them have to be studied.
5. **What is livelihood security?**
   - Livelihood includes necessary facilities, opportunities, resources, capabilities and actions to lead the life effectively.
   - Security refers to the recognition to use the resources and basic services and the ability to tackle the risks during the period of distress.
6. **What are the livelihood resources?**
   - Livelihood resources refer to the resources which provide men and women to fulfil the basic needs like food, cloth, drinking water, shelter and good health.
7. **What are the types of livelihood resources?**

   There are five types of livelihood resources. They are:
   - Natural Resources
   - Human Resources
   - Social Resources
   - Financial Resources
   - Physical Resources
8. **Mention institutions and organizations that work towards rural development**
   - Government Departments
   - Local Self-Government (Panchayats)
   - Non-Governmental Organizations (NGOs)
   - Community Based Organizations (CBOs)
   - Parallel bodies
   - Schools
   - Religious and Community Associations (RCAs)
   - Traders Guild
   - Cooperative Societies
   - Banks
   - Commercial Enterprises
   - Service Centers
   - International Donor Agencies
   - Corporate

9. What is the role of the Government in the development of a village?

- Promotion of balanced growth
- Assuring food security
- Education for all
- Employment guarantee
- Protected drinking water
- Basic infrastructure
- Medical facilities
- Agricultural growth
- Small-scale industries
- Social reforms
- Transport facilities
- Women development
- Child welfare
- Widow rehabilitation
- Self-reliance
- Multi-purpose training
- Free Legal Aid

10. What is Panchayat?

- Panchayat is an institution for governance
- A Panchayat comprises the leader and members elected by the people
- An institution that has a very close and direct relationship with the people of the village
- An institution that identifies and resolves common problems of the village within its jurisdiction
- An institution where people learn practices of democratic system of governance
- An institution which works for economic development and social justice
- An institution that identifies felt needs, prioritize and promotes the overall development of the village
- An institution which prepares plan for development.

11. What are the principles of SHGs?

- Mutual help
- Mutual trust
- Thrift and savings

- Promotion of punctuality, honesty, discipline in the transactions of the group
- Participatory credit management
- Adoption of uncorrupt practices in financial management.

12. **What are the functions of social workers in the process of rural development?**
    - Building rapport with the community
    - Gaining clear-cut knowledge about the village
    - Analyzing the problems of the village along with the villagers through participatory method
    - Arriving at solutions to the problems in a participatory mode
    - Exploring the possibilities of finding solutions to the problems with the help of the community organizations in the village
    - Planning important activities to be undertaken in the village
    - Strengthening the SHGs and youth clubs in the village
    - Proposing important activities to be undertaken in the village through Panchayat by establishing rapport with the Panchayat
    - Initiating steps to solve the problems of the people through government department
    - Serving as a clearing house of information in the village.

8. Evaluating the Performance of the Students

All the students are engaged in all the seven days. Each one has got a general task and responsibility and a specific task. How the students are discharging their roles and responsibilities have to be evaluated. Since, all the teachers are involved in the whole process, while assigning marks to the students, teachers collectively decide. In the discussion the teachers who were with the students in the field in all seven days have to play a major role in giving input. Broadly the following aspects are considered while evaluating the performance of the teachers. They are in a diagram.

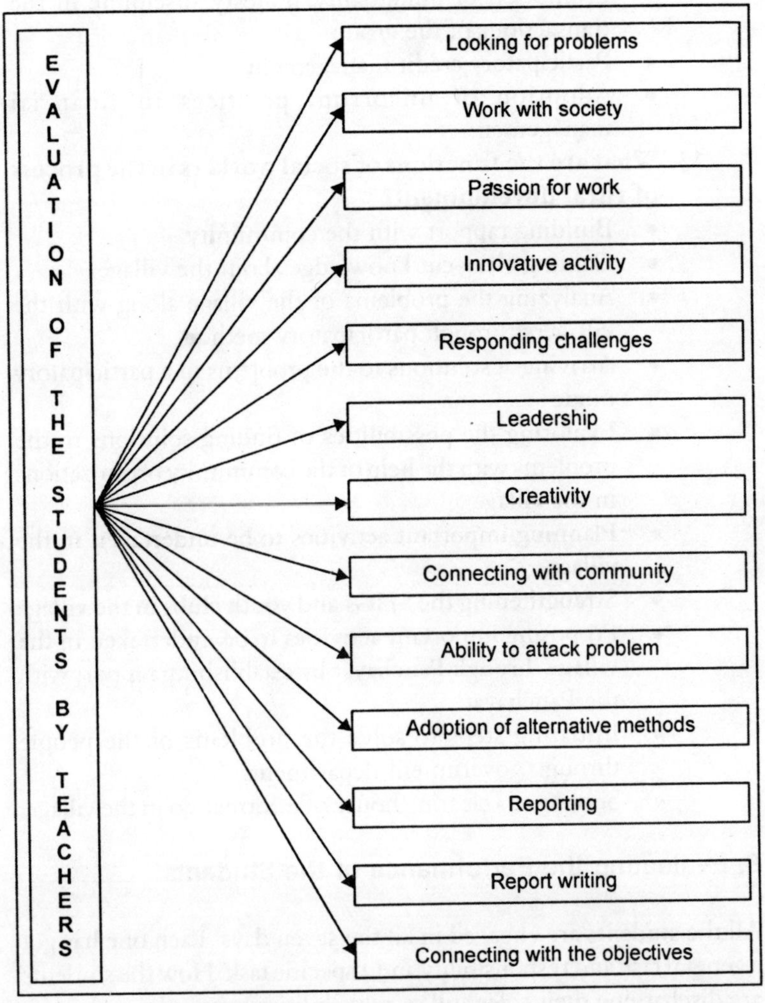
EVALUATION OF THE STUDENTS BY TEACHERS
Looking for problems
Work with society
Passion for work
Innovative activity
Responding challenges
Leadership
Creativity
Connecting with community
Ability to attack problem
Adoption of alternative methods
Reporting
Report writing
Connecting with the objectives

3
Camp Inauguration

To inaugurate the camp the teacher in charge has invited the Block Development Officers (BDO) from Aathoor Block. Regular BDO and BDO looking after Gram Panchayat have come and participated in the inaugural function. In the inaugural function the BDO looked after the Gram Panchayats, explained the schemes directly operated by the Gram Panchayats and schemes carried out by the respective line departments. While explaining the activities, he indicated the administrative difficulties involved in implementing the schemes. He specifically informed the students about the financial outlay of each scheme. He indicated the non-cooperation of the people to the government officials for failure of many of the schemes. Students have asked questions about the poor conditions of sanitation in the Dalit village. He said that the government is willing to help financially the poor to construct toilets. But people have not evinced any interest. He also requested the students to create awareness among the people about the importance of sanitation. Further, he elaborated the role of Panchayats in the socio-economic transformation of the communities. He explained succinctly the different phases of rural development activities since independence by recollecting his own experiences. He listed out the major transformation that took place in the villages over a period of time because of the several initiatives of the governments. He concluded his address by capturing the poor capacity of the local body leaders in managing the Panchayat institutions. The other BDO explained the activities of the Block Panchayats while explaining the above he traced the activities of the local bodies since independence.

Box I: Development Starts from Education

While speaking to the students the BDO asked a question "How many of you have more than one sister or one brother?" For this question only five students replied that they were born with two others. Many of the students said that they were alone in their family. A few replied that they were two. The moment he got the reply, BDO said that this small family is due to work done by the rural development functionaries in the 1950s and 1960s. He narrated his family story. He said that he was with seven brothers and sisters together. But he has only one daughter and she is a doctor got married to a surgeon. He informed that he took a decision in his family to have only one child as he was advocating small family norm as rural development functionary. He very interestingly correlated the factor education with development which starts from individual to family and family to community and community to society and society to country. He in fact requested the students to understand the facilities, services and institutions provided by the government. But they are not utilized by the communities properly.

Box II: Physical Development Vs. Human Growth

Another BDO explained to the students about the conditions in which they lived. When he was a boy, there was no school in his village, no healthcare in his village, no cooperative society in his village, no pre-primary school, no post office, no telephone, no road, no bus, no electricity, no water supply through pipes, and the whole life was in struggle. There was no ration shop and no government office in the village premises. No police station nearer to his village. That was the condition throughout the country. But now he said, there is a primary school, pre-primary school, public distribution shop, village administrative office, cooperative store, water supply system, community hall, every house telephone, every house is electrified, there are fine black top road, every small village is connected by mini bus, every house you have television set, every village is connected with primary health centre through sub health centre, every 5000 population you have a primary health centre with 24 hours doctor service with operation theatre, free 108 Ambulance service. All basic facilities are being provided by the Government. Yet why the communities are not leading a decent and dignified human life? He raised the question and asked the students to ponder over the question.

The inauguration came to an end around 1.30 p.m. with a few questions. They are:

- Huge investment in providing basic infrastructure facilities at the village level.
- Numbers of institutions have been developed at the village level over a period of time.
- Continuously plethoras of schemes have been implemented in the villages.

- Yet why we are not able to see the communities to lead a decent life? Where is the problem? For Human Development all necessary steps had been taken by the Government yet Human Development has not been achieved as Kerala has achieved.

4
Programme in Action

1. Orientation to the Students

Previous day of the Village Placement Programme an orientation programme was conducted. Students have been briefed about the basic objectives of the seven days programme. Focus was given on the benefits to be gained by the students in the whole programme. Later activities to be carried out in the village have been discussed. Students have suggested certain thrust areas on which study has to be carried out. As the village selected for Village Placement Programme is dominated by the presence of dalits, students have selected the themes related to Dalit transformation for studies in the field. Being the coordinator of the programme I have explained to the students about the deep implications of the Village Placement Programme. While explaining the implications of Village Placement Programme (VPP) what students have to do in the village had been discussed. The issues on which students have to work had been discussed and they had been finalized. I only facilitated them to suggest topics for investigation in the village during Village Placement Programme.

2. Activities

What are the activities to be carried out in the villages have been decided well in advance in the Department after making two preliminary visits to the village. I have explained the basic details of the village where the students have to stay, the students have finalized the issues to be studied while they will be in the camp. There are certain activities which are basic and mandatory. Everyday Morning Prayer has to be conducted. It should be always an inter-religious prayer. It is not only for the benefit of the students but also for the benefit of the villagers. People in the villages should be exposed on the importance of inter-religious prayer. Normally, when our students perform inter-religious prayer in the open ground, villagers used to observe and make enquiries about the need of such prayer. Students used to explain the importance and implications of such prayer in the context of increasing conflict among the collectivities based on religion. After the prayer manual activities will be carried out in the camp site (Shramdaan), primarily they clean the premises everyday and along with the above, in all public places wherever they find filth they are being cleaned. This manual work is being carried out not for the benefit of the villagers and it is for the benefit of the students. Students should internalize the importance of the manual work.

Groups have been formed among the students. One set of groups meant for village studies another set of groups are meant for camp management. Every day time is allotted for group discussion, report preparation, presentation of report and review of camp management. Below given programme schedule and time table is self-evident for the activities,

While making presentation of reports everyday teachers will be there to bring clarity to the discussion. Students used to participate in the discussion. They raise questions, add points for discussion, and make observation and so on. Students used to enjoy the process. During the presentations students exhibit the photographs which they have taken during the process of data collection.

3. Programme Schedule

Sl. No.	Day	Daily Works	Time
1	**Day I 14.12.2013**	Prayer	6.00 am to 7.00 am
		Shramdaan	7.00 am to 8.30 am
		Breakfast, Refreshment and Discussion	8.30 am to 10.00 am
		Data Collection	10.00 am to 12.00 am
		Discussion	12.00 am to 1.00 pm
		Lunch	1.00 pm to 2.00 pm
		Discussion	2.00 pm to 3.30 pm
		Refreshment	3.30 pm to 4.00 pm
		Data Collection	4.00 pm to 6.00 pm
		Report Writing	6.00 pm to 7.00 pm
		Dinner	7.00 pm to 8.30 pm
		Presentation	8.30 pm to 9.30 pm
		Cultural Activities	9.30 pm to 10.00 pm
2	**Day II 15.12.2013**	Prayer	6.00 am to 7.00 am
		Shramdaan	7.00 am to 8.30 am
		Breakfast, Refreshment and Discussion	8.30 am to 10.00 am
		Data Collection	10.00 am to 12.00 am
		Discussion	12.00 am to 1.00 pm
		Lunch	1.00 pm to 2.00 pm
		Discussion	2.00 pm to 3.30 pm
		Refreshment	3.30 pm to 4.00 pm
		Data Collection	4.00 pm to 6.00 pm
		Report Writing	6.00 pm to 7.00 pm
		Dinner	7.00 pm to 8.30 pm
		Presentation	8.30 pm to 9.30 pm
		Cultural Activities	9.30 pm to 10.00 pm
	Day III 16.12.2013	Prayer	6.00 am to 7.00 am
		Shramdaan	7.00 am to 8.30 am
		Breakfast, Refreshment and Discussion	8.30 am to 10.00 am
		Data Collection	10.00 am to 12.00 am
		Discussion	12.00 am to 1.00 pm

Sl. No.	*Day*	*Daily Works*	*Time*
		Lunch	1.00 pm to 2.00 pm
		Discussion	2.00 pm to 3.30 pm
		Refreshment	3.30 pm to 4.00 pm
		Data Collection	4.00 pm to 6.00 pm
		Report Writing	6.00 pm to 7.00 pm
		Dinner	7.00 pm to 8.30 pm
		Presentation	8.30 pm to 9.30 pm
		Cultural Activities	9.30 pm to 10.00 pm
	Day IV	Prayer	6.00 am to 7.00 am
	17.12.2013	Shramdaan	7.00 am to 8.30 am
		Breakfast, Refreshment and Discussion	8.30 am to 10.00 am
		Data Collection	10.00 am to 12.00 am
		Discussion	12.00 am to 1.00 pm
		Lunch	1.00 pm to 2.00 pm
		Discussion	2.00 pm to 3.30 pm
		Refreshment	3.30 pm to 4.00 pm
		Data Collection	4.00 pm to 6.00 pm
		Report Writing	6.00 pm to 7.00 pm
		Dinner	7.00 pm to 8.30 pm
		Presentation	8.30 pm to 9.30 pm
		Cultural Activities	9.30 pm to 10.00 pm
	Day V	Prayer	6.00 am to 7.00 am
	18.12.2013	Shramdaan	7.00 am to 8.30 am
		Breakfast, Refreshment and Discussion	8.30 am to 10.00 am
		Data Collection	10.00 am to 12.00 am
		Discussion	12.00 am to 1.00 pm
		Lunch	1.00 pm to 2.00 pm
		Discussion	2.00 pm to 3.30 pm
		Refreshment	3.30 pm to 4.00 pm
		Data Collection	4.00 pm to 6.00 pm
		Report Writing	6.00 pm to 7.00 pm
		Dinner	7.00 pm to 8.30 pm
		Presentation	8.30 pm to 9.30 pm
		Cultural Activities	9.30 pm to 10.00 pm

Sl. No.	*Day*	*Daily Works*	*Time*
	Day VI	Prayer	6.00 am to 7.00 am
	19.12.2013	Shramdaan	7.00 am to 8.30 am
		Breakfast, Refreshment and Discussion	8.30 am to 10.00 am
		Data Collection	10.00 am to 12.00 am
		Discussion	12.00 am to 1.00 pm
		Lunch	1.00 pm to 2.00 pm
		Discussion	2.00 pm to 3.30 pm
		Refreshment	3.30 pm to 4.00 pm
		Data Collection	4.00 pm to 6.00 pm
		Report Writing	6.00 pm to 7.00 pm
		Dinner	7.00 pm to 8.30 pm
		Presentation	8.30 pm to 9.30 pm
		Cultural Activities	9.30 pm to 10.00 pm
	Day VII	Prayer	6.00 am to 7.00 am
	20.12.2013	Shramdaan	7.00 am to 8.30 am
		Breakfast, Refreshment and Discussion	8.30 am to 10.00 am
		Data Collection	10.00 am to 12.00 am
		Discussion	12.00 am to 1.00 pm
		Lunch	1.00 pm to 2.00 pm
		Discussion	2.00 pm to 3.30 pm
		Refreshment	3.30 pm to 4.00 pm
		Data Collection	4.00 pm to 6.00 pm
		Report Writing	6.00 pm to 7.00 pm
		Dinner	7.00 pm to 8.30 pm
		Presentation	8.30 pm to 9.30 pm
		Cultural Activities	9.30 pm to 10.00 pm

4. Group Activities

Groups have been formed for studying various aspects of the community life in the rural setting. Groups have been assigned the details of activities.

Group Activities

Sl. No	Assignment	Details of the Assignment	Group Leader	Members
1.	Activities of Panchayat	Panchayat activities have to be studied and for which the students have to interact with the elected representatives and the people. Focus could be given on service delivery of Panchayat and the problems faced by the Panchayat while performing the duties and responsibilities of the Panchayat.	Gokul Raja, P.	Manikandan, S. Ponmanikandan, R. Periya Samy, P. Leosimon, U.
2.	Expectation from the Government, Panchayat and MLA/MP	Students have to study the role expectation of the people from the multiple representatives representing the people in three different Governments namely Local Government, State Government and Central Government. Primarily it is designed with an objective of understanding the people's perception about the roles to be performed by the representatives of the people in local bodies, state legislature and national parliament	Loganathan, N.	Nithya, M. Prabu, P. Udayakumar, P. Jeyaraj, S.

(*Contd.*)

(Contd.)

Sl. No.	Assignment	Details of the Assignment	Group Leader	Members
3.	Livelihood Conditions of the Poor	This group has to study the livelihood conditions of the people. The problems faced by the poor and the governments support through the scheme have to be studied. Focus could be given on the gaps in the schemes.	Thangavel, K.	Muthumariammal, P. Nithyapriya, M. Ovammal, G. Shargunam, S.
4.	Opportunities for Entrepreneurship	Exploring the opportunities for entrepreneurship in the village setting in the given background of National Capital, Human Capital, Economic Capital and Social Capital.	Yagavalli, G.	Indu, M.S. Renugadevi, N. Jayarakshmi, S. Shanmugavel, S.
5.	Corruption in Governance	This group has to study how corrupt practices have affected the poor and suggest various measures to reduce corruption. It has to be seen from the perspective of middle men between the government and the community.	Kuralarasan, P.	Senthilkumar, C. Swathika Meenakshi, T. Enees Diana, S. Akshaya Divakaran

(Contd.)

(Contd.)

Sl. No.	Assignment	Details of the Assignment	Group Leader	Members
6.	Infrastructure – Public Toilet, School, PDS and Rural Library	An assessment has to be made about the available infrastructure, their conditions and their utility.	Ashok, M.	Sathya, K Premalatha, V. Arunraj, A.
7.	Case study – Rich Person	This group has to study the process of wealth making in the village itself by conducting a few case studies. Basic principles or factors that worked in the process of wealth making have to be studied.	Athul, S.G.	Manokaran, P. Lingeswaran, V. Brindha Devi, A. Shophia Jency, Rani
8.	Voting responsibility of voters	This group has to study the voting responsibility of the citizens by focusing its attention on the people's perception and performance. It has to be seen in the present context of cash for votes.	Hepsiba, V.	Nisha, S. Banu, J. Sreejith Karthick, M.

(Contd.)

(Contd.)

Sl. No.	*Assignment*	*Details of the Assignment*	*Group Leader*	*Members*
9.	Conflict Management	Focus could be given on the conflict management practices available in the village. Primarily the group has to study the process of managing the conflicts in the villages. Institutional rules and practices have to be studied.	Saravana-kumar, C.	Balamurugan, B Padmavathy, B Gautham, P Ramya, T
10.	Conditions of Sanitation	Sanitary conditions of the village have to be studied. The real reasons for the poor sanitary conditions have to be studied.	Arunmani Pandiyan, M.	Karthika, A. Dinesh, R. Raja, S. Lingammal.
11.	Social Relationship	Since it is a Dalit dominated village, social relationship among the caste groups have to be studied by this group of students.	Gowthami, S.	Hyma Suresh, K. Surya, S. Thangamani, N. Bushra Aabeetha, M. Manikandan, S.

(Contd.)

(*Contd.*)

Sl. No.	*Assignment*	*Details of the Assignment*	*Group Leader*	*Members*
12.	Problems of Single Family and Poor Family	Problems of the single member family have to be studied by this group. This issue has to be seen in the backdrop of the social security schemes.	Karthik Varun, A.	Manikandan, S. Pavithraa, R. Dhanapal, S. Ninglum Keishing
13.	Conditions of Dalits	Since there are three groups of Dalits in this village, general conditions of them have to be studied.	Rengapandi, C.	Everest Robert, P. Kalpana, N. Jenifer Priyanka, G. Jeeva Gowsick, J.E.
14.	Health Conditions of Women	Health conditions of children and women have to be studied by this group.	Sindhu, G.	Sasipriya, R. Rajalakshmi, M.P. Sreelakshmi, M.P. Balamurugan, R.
15.	Skills Available	Skills available in this village and their employability have to be studied by this group from the perspective of demographic dividend.	Manisha Shree, R.	Sarmila, P. Jeyapradap, V Vouvanathi, C Kasthuri

(*Contd.*)

(Contd.)

Sl. No.	*Assignment*	*Details of the Assignment*	*Group Leader*	*Members*
16.	Educational Status of Weaker Section	Education status of weaker section has to be studied by this group.	Aanchal Nair	Boovizhi, K. Sirajtheen, S. Vathsala, S. Sureshpandi, S.

Since the students have undergone a course on Research methodology, they can fix the tools for data collection. Students are free to evolve methodological nuances to generate data from the respondents in the village. Varieties of methods and tools have been used for this purpose.

5. Committees with Responsibilities

Committees have been formed among the students to manage the camp. The students have to manage themselves and carry out certain activities for the camp. Details are given below:

Committees with Responsibilities

Name of Committee	*Committees with Responsibilities*	*Group leader*	*Members*
Food and Accommodation Committee	It is responsibility of the committee for preparation, and food distribution. By helping the cook by many ways cost of preparation of food has to be reduced. Entire food preparation and distribution have to be done by this group.	Gowthami, S.	Karthikvarun, A. Indu, M.S. Manikandan, S. Renugadevi, N. Everest Robert, P. Balamurugan, B. Padmavathy, B. Gautham, P. Ramya, T.
Programme and Management Committee	This committee supervises the overall programme. Adherences to time and carrying out the activities with almost sincerity and seriousness have to be ensured.	Sindhu, G.	Nithya, M. Sarmila, P. Bushra Aabeetha, M. Nisha, S. Jinni, M.N.
Photography	This group is entrusted with a responsibility of taking photographs in the camp sites while the students are in action.	Athul, S.G.	Prabu, P. Sureshpandi, S. Muthumariammal, P. Nithyapriya, M.

(*Contd.*)

(Contd.)

Name of Committee	*Committees with Responsibilities*	*Group leader*	*Members*
Power Point Presentation Committee	This committee has to get points from the groups to prepare Power Point presentation to be made in review.	Manish Shree, R.	Yagavalli, G. Sreelakshmi, M.P. Pavithraa, R. Brindha Devi, A. Hyama Suresh Thangamani, N.
Report Writing Committee	This committee has to take responsibility for preparing the report of the whole exercises.	Aanchal Nair	Karthikvarun, A. Rajalakshmi, M.P. Boovizhi, L. Karthika Premalatha, V. Akshaya Divakaran
Discipline Committee	Discipline has to be maintained and for which the committee has to work.	Gokul Raja, P.	Arunmani Pandiyan, M. Karthika, V. Dinesh, R. Raja, S. Jeyapradap, V. Vouvanathi Kasthuri, C. Sasipriya, R

(Contd.)

(*Contd.*)

Name of Committee	*Committees with Responsibilities*	*Group leader*	*Members*
Culture and Shramadaan Committee	For shramdaan and cultural activities, this committee has to take efforts on each day	Rengapandi, C.	Muthumariammal, P. Leosimon, U. Jeeva Gowsick, J.E. Aravinraj, M. Ovammal, G. Sureshpandi, S.

5
Programme Reporting

1. Profile of the Village

Palayankottai Panchayat is divided into nine wards, and students have concentrated their study in three wards. This panchayat has a population of about 3255. It has got a complex caste system. The panchayat is dominated by the presence of the scheduled caste that includes *Parayar, Pallar, Arunthathiyar* (chakliar). The BCs include *Maniyakar* as the most prevalent while there is also a *Chettiyar* family. The MBCs include *Naykar* community who are present in a fair number. Backward Class and Most Backward Class families are very less in number.

Palayankottai Panchayat

GENERAL PROFILE

State: Tamil Nadu

District: Dindigul

Union: Athoor

Taluk: Athoor

Clerk: P. Balraj

Gram Panchayat

President: A. Sumathi Balamurugan (suspended and BDO is in charge)
Vice President: S. Nagaraj

Ward Members

1. M. Sunmugam
2. G. Maanikkam
3. P. Balamurgan
4. N. Then Mozhi
5. S. Nagaraj
6. T. Mansulla
7. G. Palaniammal
8. R. Kannan
9. A. Gomathi

Villages in the Panchayat

1. Palayankottai
2. Piravanpatti
3. Sedapatti
4. Oldkammanpaati
5. Koolampaati
6. Kannimarnagar
7. Lakshmipuram

Castes in the Panchayat

1. Maniyar
2. Chttiyar
3. Nayakkar
4. Pallar
5. Vannar
6. Amattayar
7. Arunthathiyar
8. Parayar
9. Konar
10. Bhramin
11. Vellalar

Basic Details

Total Population: 3250
Households: 816
Voters: 1212
Post Office: 1

Library: 1
Health Centre: 1
Grossary Shop: 1
Community Hall: 1
Open Air Theater: 1
Anganwadi: 6
Public Toilets: 1
Temples: 45
Roads: Cement road and black topped roads
Sintex Tank: 17
Street Light: 100
Water Tap: 100
Village Administration Office: 1
SHG Building: 1
Youth Club: 1

2. Education as Factor in Development

An excellent rapport was created among the people of the village where our students stayed. The prime task before the students was to understand the level of awareness among the people about the role of education in the process of development. It is a Dalit village and the parents are not so rich and yet the importance given to education is unimaginable. Every family belong to the Dalit community had a resolve to educate their children whether they are boys and girls. How they got such a resolve is a riddle. The curious question here is to what extent they take steps to educate their kids? A group of students went to different families interacted with the responsible available in the house during the visit of our students in the village. Of the 16 respondents 6 are women. The students went to the houses of the respondents with six questions. In the same families, our students interacted with school going boys and girls. 15 school going boys and girls were interviewed and of them five were girls. They were asked to give reply to five questions as their parents. The whole interaction took place for an hour and half in each family. All the respondents are educated. They have determined to educate their children. While doing so, they even do not mind to pay from their hard earned money to the private school to educate their kids. They have a clear-cut perception that by giving good education to their kids, they feel that the whole family will be transformed. They have interested such a transformation in many of the families in their own villages. Perhaps they have seen such a transformation in the globalization era. The school going boys and girls are also having the same perception that by their education they have determined to transform their family. Their aspiration to achieve development is very high. The schools whether public, private have got all basic facilities.

Box III: They are the Hopes

A few school going boys used to come to the camp site everyday in the evening and during day time on Sunday also to interact with our boys and girls out of curiosity. The boys are cute, well dressed, and clean neat and they are belonging to Dalit families. One cannot decipher unless they inform they are from the Dalit families. When they were with our boys in the camp I curiousily noted their questions and interactions with our students. After seeing their communication ability I called them along with my students and interacted with them. Of the boys barring two all are studying in private English Medium schools. When they were asked about their life goal everyone said that they wanted to be an IAS officer, IFS officer, Doctor, and Engineer. Further they responded that they wanted to migrate from the village to other places to get gainful employment opportunity. Subsequently I asked about their parents. They informed that they are from the families of daily wage earner. No one has got land and everybody is a coolie. It created curiosity in me and I wanted to interact with their parents. One boy immediately identified very near to our camp site his mother. I interacted with her. My question to her was "why you are spending so much for the education of your son in the private schools when there are public schools." She immediately replied that the quality of education is high and fine in private schools. Moreover, we want to end the pattern of life we lead to-day to my son. Let him lead a decent and dignified human life anywhere other than this place. She further informed that they are struggling in their life to earn money to educate their only son. I asked another related question. Can you provide the same to all your children? She said that she has only two. Another one child is girl. She wanted to groom her as a staff nurse. She further informed me that in this village the Dalit families very rarely will have three kids. Majority of the Dalit families either they have one or two children. A very few families are having more than two kids. The whole interaction gave me the hope that life of Dalit will be transformed through the instrument of education.

Table 5.1: Responses of Parents on Education

Sl. No.	*Name*	*Sex*	*Are you educated?*		*Are your children educated?*		*If girls, are they educated?*		*Type of school where they study*		*If private total amount spent annually?*
			SSLC	*Higher education*	*Yes*	*No*	*Yes*	*No*	*Govt.*	*Private*	
1	Mageshwari	Female	✓	—	✓	—	—	—	✓	—	—
2	Murugan	Male	✓	—	✓	—	✓	—	—	✓	17,000
3	Velusamy	Male	—	✓	✓	—	—	—	✓	—	—
4	Ajith Kumar	Male	✓	—	✓	—	✓			✓	20,000
5	Rajkumar	Male	✓		✓				✓		
6	Irrulayee	Female		✓	✓				✓		
7	Manokari	Female		✓	✓		✓		✓		
8	Jayalakshmi	Female	✓		✓				✓		
9	Thamariselven	Male		✓	✓					✓	18,000
10	Aryamala	Female		✓	✓		✓		✓		
11	Balamurugan	Male	✓		✓		✓			✓	20,000
12	Kausalya	Female		✓	✓		✓		✓		
13	Saravanakumar	Male	✓		✓		✓		✓		
14	Sriraman	Male	✓		✓		✓		✓		
15	Kannaiya	Male	✓		✓		✓			✓	20,000

Source: Computed.

Conclusion

Value of education has gone in to the minds of people. They have a feeling that through the instrument, a family could get maximum benefits from poverty alleviation to achieving prosperity. The state government schemes such as providing cycles and laptops have enormously helped the students to go for higher education. Our general observation was that everyone wanted their children to be educated. They felt that education will help to remove the stigma often associated to minority groups

3. Sanitation

Introduction

This study is based on the sanitation conditions in the Palayankottai village. Our preliminary observation through transact walk reveals that the sanitary conditions are very poor in the village. We found that open defecation is rampant in the village. Drainage system is not present and where it was present, it was unclean and dirty. Moreover, there was only one public toilet and that too for women. We also found that most of the houses did not have toilet facilities. Hence, a study was conducted on the assumption that a sanitary condition in Palayankottai village is poor. After the students reached the village, they visited all the hamlets and took photographs of the sanitary conditions. The students have come to a conclusion that the sanitary condition is very poor. In this regard they wanted to interact with the people of the village. So a team of students went into different houses and interacted with the people. The respondents are both men and women. The primary objective of the interaction was to find out the awareness level of the people about sanitation. The students have interacted with the respondents on the facilities available and the maintenance of the facilities. Students who have interacted with the respondents concluded that there is no awareness about sanitation and water supply. People having toilets and water tap in their houses informed that they are in good condition. Others have responded that the conditions of sanitation are bad.

Table 5.2: Responses of the Public towards Water Supply

Sl. No.	*Name*	*Sex*	*Age*	*Education level*	*Water facility*		*Water availability*	
					Good	*Bad*	*Good*	*Bad*
1.	Mageshwari	Female	32	Primary	✓	–	✓	–
2.	Murugan	Male	38	Secondary	–	✓	–	✓
3.	Velusamy	Male	65	Illiterate	✓	–	✓	✓
4.	Ajith Kumar	Male	18	Secondary	–	✓	✓	–
5.	Rajkumar	Male	22	Graduate	–	✓	–	✓
6.	Irrulayee	Female	56	Illiterate	✓	–	–	✓
7.	Manokari	Female	23	Secondary	–	✓	✓	–
8.	Jayalakshmi	Female	10	Primary	✓	–	–	✓
9.	Thamariselven	Male	28	Secondary	–	✓	–	✓
10.	Aryamala	Female	60	Illiterate	✓	–	✓	✓
11.	Balamurugan	Male	31	Secondary	–	✓	–	✓
12.	Kausalya	Female	21	Secondary	✓	–	–	✓
13.	Saravana Kumar	Male	25	Secondary	–	✓	✓	–
14.	Sriraman	Male	7	Primary	–	✓	✓	–
15.	Kannaiya	Male	55	Illiterate	–	✓	–	✓
16.	Karuppayya	Male	7	Primary	✓	–	✓	–
17.	Pugalenthi	Male	13	Primary	–	✓	–	✓
18.	Mahamayee	Female	23	Illiterate	–	✓	–	✓
19.	Mariyapan	Male	30	Primary	–	✓	–	✓
20.	Muniraja	Male	11	Primary	✓	–	✓	–
21.	Manivasagam	Male	11	Primary	✓	–	✓	–
22.	Ponnalagu	Female	45	Illiterate	–	✓	–	✓
23.	Selvi	Female	35	Secondary	✓	–	✓	–
24.	Priya	Female	28	Secondary	–	✓	✓	–
25.	Siva Raj	Male	31	Illiterate	–	✓	–	✓

Source: Computed.

Table 5.3: Responses of the Public towards Toilet Facilities

Sl. No.	*Name*	*Sex*	*Age*	*Education level*	*Toilet facility*		*Toilet availability*	
					Good	*Bad*	*Good*	*Bad*
1.	Mageshwari	Female	32	Primary	✓	–	✓	–
2.	Murugan	Male	38	Secondary	–	✓	–	✓
3.	Velusamy	Male	65	Illiterate	–	✓	–	✓
4.	Ajith Kumar	Male	18	Secondary	✓	–	✓	–
5.	Rajkumar	Male	22	Graduate	–	✓	–	✓
6.	Irrulayee	Female	56	Illiterate	–	✓	–	✓
7.	Manokari	Female	23	Secondary	–	✓	✓	–
8.	Jayalakshmi	Female	10	Primary	✓		–	✓
9.	Thamariselven	Male	28	Secondary	–	✓	–	✓
10.	Aryamala	Female	60	Illiterate	✓	–	✓	✓
11.	Balamurugan	Male	31	Secondary	–	✓	–	✓
12.	Kausalya	Female	21	Secondary	✓	–	–	✓
13.	Saravana Kumar	Male	25	Secondary	–	✓	✓	–

(Contd.)

Table 5.3 (*Contd.*)

Sl. No.	*Name*	*Sex*	*Age*	*Education level*	*Toilet facility*		*Toilet availability*	
					Good	*Bad*	*Good*	*Bad*
14.	Sriraman	Male	7	Primary	–	✓	✓	–
15.	Kannaiya	Male	55	Illiterate	–	✓	–	✓
16.	Karuppayya	Male	7	Primary	✓	–	✓	–
17.	Pogalenthi	Male	13	Primary	–	✓	–	✓
18.	Mahamayee	Female	23	Illiterate	–	✓	–	✓
19.	Mariyapan	Male	30	Primary	–	✓	–	✓
20.	Muniraja	Male	11	Primary	✓	–	✓	–
21.	Manivasagam	Male	11	Primary	✓	–	✓	–
22.	Ponnalagu	Female	45	Illiterate	–	✓	–	✓
23.	Selvi	Female	35	Secondary	✓	–	✓	–
24.	Priya	Female	28	Secondary	–	✓	✓	–
25.	Siva Raj	Male	31	Illiterate	–	✓	–	✓

Source: Computed.

Table 5.4: Responses of the Public towards Drainage Facilities

Sl. No.	*Name*	*Sex*	*Age*	*Education level*	*Drainage facility*		*Drainage maintenance*	
					Good	*Bad*	*Good*	*Bad*
1.	Mageshwari	Female	32	Primary	✓	–	✓	–
2.	Murugan	Male	38	Secondary		✓	–	✓
3.	Velusamy	Male	65	Illiterate	✓	✓	✓	✓
4.	Ajith Kumar	Male	18	Secondary	–	✓	✓	–
5.	Rajkumar	Male	22	Graduate	–	✓	–	✓
6.	Irrulayee	Female	56	Illiterate	✓	–	–	✓
7.	Manokari	Female	23	Secondary	–	✓	✓	–
8.	Jayalakshmi	Female	10	Primary	✓	–	–	✓
9.	Thamariselven	Male	28	Secondary	–	✓	–	✓
10.	Aryamala	Female	60	Illiterate	✓	–	✓	✓
11.	Balamurugan	Male	31	Secondary	–	✓	–	✓
12.	Kausalya	Female	21	Secondary	✓	–	–	✓
13.	Saravana Kumar	Male	25	Secondary	–	✓	✓	–
14.	Sriraman	Male	7	Primary	–	✓	✓	–
15.	Kannaiya	Male	55	Illiterate	–	✓	–	✓
16.	Karuppayya	Male	7	Primary	✓	–	✓	–
17.	Pugalenthi	Male	13	Primary	–	✓	–	✓
18.	Mahamayee	Female	23	Illiterate	–	✓	–	✓
19.	Mariyapan	Male	30	Primary	–	✓	–	✓
20.	Muniraja	Male	11	Primary	✓	–	✓	–
21.	Manivasagam	Male	11	Primary	✓	–	✓	–
22.	Ponnalagu	Female	45	Illiterate	–	✓	–	✓
23.	Selvi	Female	35	Secondary	✓	–	✓	–
24.	Priya	Female	28	Secondary	–	✓	✓	–
25.	Siva Raj	Male	31	Illiterate	–	✓	–	✓

Source: Computed.

Some of the well meaning people felt that there is no proper maintenance of streets, and sewage facilities. Everywhere people put filth and they are not properly treated. Nobody has got solution to solve the problems. When government gave money Panchayat has constructed toilets for women. But they are not properly maintained. With regard to water supply nobody knows the quality of water they get for drinking purposes. Neither the Panchayats nor the health departments bother to test the water quality which is being used by the people in the village. Water is being pumped, stored and distributed through pipes. People do not have any idea of clean water. They think that water comes through pipes is clean.

Box IV: School Boys on Sanitation

Boys, who are studying in private schools, came to us for interaction. They were intelligent boys. They had clear-cut ideas about goals and life ambition. When we saw that they were going in open air for defecation, we brought them to our camp site and we interacted with them. Their reply was a shock for us. They told us about the implications of open air defecation as experts. They got all the details from the books. They practice sanitation in the school but not in house as their parents did not listen to their arguments. They further explained to us that they do reluctantly because of the instruction of their parents. When we asked a question how you will construct a house if you want to construct a house on your own. All the kids said that they will construct house with toilets. They unequivocally said that they will migrate from this village while they go for job and they will construct good houses. "When you have such sensitivity why you are not able to sensitize your parents?" was our next question. They said that they failed miserably in this regard. They in fact asked us to interact with their parents. The whole interaction with the boys about sanitary conditions gave us hope that the conditions will improve in another ten years.

Box V: Their Parents on Sanitation

Interestingly we interacted with their parents. Of them one responded by bringing the facts to us. He argued that everybody talks about toilets. We do agree with them that toilets are very essential for sanitation. Where is water for toilets? Even for bathing, and for cleaning vessels we have to travel one kilometer to fetch water. For drinking water I have to wait in a queue and for that also we have to travel for one kilometer. Everyday people are spending at least two hours to fetch water for our daily use. Further during the time of power shortage we have to spend more time. We do not have enough quantity of water to the level of our requirement to use water in the toilets. Has anyone consulted the people what is the appropriate method to maintain sanitation in the village? Nobody has done that exercise. The above arguments were projected by a gentleman from this village. If we are in a position to provide water supply very nearer to the houses to the level of requirement, there is no problem in constructing toilets.

Box VI: More Temples in the Village have Poor Sanitation

It is a Dalit village and it has got nine temples and all were built by the people through their contributions. Annually they conduct temple festivals for all the nine temples. On an average every temple needs Rs. 3 to Rs. 5 lakh for the annual temple festivals. They celebrate the festivals by collecting money from the people.

When they spent huge money for temples, they could not spare a small amount Rs. 900 to construct a toilet. Rs. 11000 is being given by the government for constructing toilets in the houses. For individual house they provide toilets. In the entire village every house has at least one cell phone and a TV set. This scenario has created a puzzle for our students. When the Block Development Officer came, he requested our students to take steps to sensitize people on sanitation. We did that exercise in this village through street play and one consultative street workshop on 'development'. When a student highlighted the implications of open air defecation everyone started telling that the priority of them now is sanitation. Further yet another student informed them that even the 900 rupees they need not spend instead they can do work for constructing the toilet for their houses through the MGNREGA. Every family can get one toilet free of cost. The entire village is going to be fully sanitised village. This happens because of a smaller intervention by the students.

Box VII: Awareness Creation for Sanitation

As a part of the Village Placement Programme for the academic year 2013-14, the students of MA (5 year Integrated) Development Administration of the Department of Political Science and Development Administration, Gandhigram Rural Institute performed a street play in Palayankottai village in the Dindigul District. The theme of the street play was fixed as sanitation and hygiene of the people as students found that village lacks proper sanitation and there was rampant open defecation. The play was scheduled during the evening when all the villagers were available and back from their day's work. A common ground in the centre of the village was selected for conducting the act. A traditional musical instrument "*Parai*" was used by the students in the play. The students went around the village beating the *Parai* which was done to inform the villagers that a play is going to be conducted in the village. The play started when villagers gathered around 9 'O' clock in the night. A welcome song was sung by students to welcome the villagers to the programme. Then in order to get the attention of the people a small drama filled with satire and comedy was performed. The drama of a deaf family really entertained the people for a few minutes. After this, a drama on the importance of toilet and hygiene was performed. Through this drama students conveyed the message that toilets are as much important like the temples in the life of the people. The intervals in between the dramas were filled by the beats of *Parai* which entertained the people. Children and youth danced to the beats of the *Parai*. Then another drama on importance of toilets and how to avail the grant of Rs 11500 provided by the government for building toilets was conveyed by means of conversations in drama. Also the

Contd....

importance of washing hands before eating, the diseases spread by unhygienic environment caused by open defecation and the threats involved in the life of the villagers were conveyed cutting across different age groups. Thus the play came to an end around 11 'O' clock. From the feedback of the people we could understand that this play and the messages were really helpful to the villagers.

Box VIII: PPT on Personal Hygiene

While seeing the school going children the students of our university found that many of the students lack awareness on personal hygiene. They have decided to create awareness among the students on personal hygiene. Since students have the skill to prepare Power Point presentation, they prepared a very effective presentation with the help of the teachers. They created in such a way that it would attract the students. Lot of pictures taken from their village have been used in the Power Point presentation. Along with a good animation was also added. The students of our institute went to the Head Master and sought his permission. With the permission of the Head Master a presentation was given to the students very effectively. Students have asked questions about the details of how to keep their houses clean and neat. It was well appreciated by the teachers and parents. The parents wanted such a kind of programme to their wards periodically on development issues.

Box IX: People are at the Receiving End

When the students of our institute involved in cleaning the premises of the community hall where students stayed, some of the villagers have opposed it. As a coordinator of the programme I wanted to know the reason for opposition to cleanliness. Someone suggested me to contact a few who keep their milch animals nearer to the community hall. I interacted with a few old men sitting very nearer to the community hall. They argued that people led their life as they perceive and the conditions which they inherit and provided to them. To change their life as government want what the government has to do are the following:

(a) Let them listen to them first.
(b) Let the government officials respect them as they have also thinking power.
(c) Let the government officials should not come with schemes with rules and strict conditions.
(d) The government officials have to listen to the people's problem and to solve the problems and for which they have to modify the schemes.
(e) While providing facilities, to maintain the facilities there should be a budget provision. And in the absence of the same what people will do?
(f) People especially the poor that too the Dalits have internalized the life in sub human living conditions.
(g) We have been seeing huge money is being wasted in the name of schemes. Government officials spent money as they have in schemes. People's basic needs are unmet.

Box X: Villagers Exploited

Muniandi, a keen observer aged 74 called me to his place in the village where we have conducted Village Placement Programme. I went to his place. He asked a question as how to stop exploitation of the villagers by outsiders. I asked him to explain the question further. He told me that from the village, poor villagers produce vegetables and paddy and grow milch animals, and goats. Villagers nurture chicken. They get eggs. They produce some products by using their skills. All the products have to be sold only in the urban areas. They are being transported to the nearest town for selling the products. All vegetables are perishable. Price for all the products are fixed by them. The villagers had no option but to sell them. When villagers demanded input for their agriculture, the price of input materials has been determined by the traders who sell fertiliser and pesticides. The wage for the farm workers is determined by the government. The life of villagers is in the hands of the people who live in urban areas. How to avoid this kind of exploitation of the villagers by the urban traders?

4. Conditions of Dalits

Introduction

Indian caste systems are unique in nature. Varieties of castes are available and the people are divided on the basis of caste, religion, culture, region and language. Nine different caste groups are found in this village. Among those there are four castes which belong to SCs. They are Pallar, Parayar, Arunthathiyar and Vannar. Through this study we are trying to find out the condition of Dalits based on social and economic conditions.

Pallar Community

Pallar community is the dominant caste in this village. Presently, 850 (eight hundred and fifty) Pallar households are in this village.

All children from this caste go to school, above 50 adolescents go to college and above 200 members from this caste are government servant which include doctors, IFS officers, etc. Some youngsters are determined to join civil service and hence they are preparing for the examinations. In comparison to the other two castes, the pallar community is having higher literacy among its people. The Pallar community gives preference to education and sends their children to study in matriculation and convents. They realize the worth of education.

The economic condition is equally good as their educational status is high. 90 per cent people of Pallar community in this village own land. People cultivate paddy, flowers, millets, coconut and vegetables. People who do not own land work as agricultural labourers and may also go for MGNREGA work. Women in this village work in nearby spinning mills.

Politically Pallar community is identified with a Dalit party "Puthiya Thamilagam". 90 per cent of them belong to that party and rest identified with DMK and AIADMK.

Pallar community has number of temples in this village but there is only one common temple in the village for which tax is collected from the Pallar community only.

Parayar Community

Parayar community is a minority like Arunthathiyar. There are only twelve families presently living in this village that belongs to Parayar community. From this community all children go to school and there is no dropout. Four adolescent boys and girls go to college. All children go to public school.

Their economic status is also fairly good. Some owns agriculture land whereas others are self-employed, such as, tailors and masons.

There is no discrimination among Parayar and Arunthathiyar communities. The Parayar community and Ampalathar (BC) community join together in conducting temple festival. Tax is not levied from Parayar community for conducting these festivals since they work for the temple. People from parayar community politically identified themselves with the AIADMK and the DMK.

Arunthathiyar Community

The Arunthathiyar community is very poor in economic condition. They work for the Pallar community which is the dominant caste in this village. This community people work mostly as agricultural labourers.

From the past Arunthathiyar community has been working for the dominant caste groups and still they work for them. This may look like caste discrimination but it is because of their poor economic condition. They work as labourers for dominant community including Pallar.

They earn about 150 rupees per day. They go to both agricultural and non-agricultural labour works. Some go to nearby mills for labour work. All the people in this caste own a house.

All the children go to the nearby public school. Only one girl child goes to Nagalakshmi Matriculation School which is nearby.

Three adolescents go to college. Only three people in this community possess a government job (Thalayari, TASMAC worker and Compounder). This community does not have any community political party. They prefer to vote for AIADMK.

The Arunthathiyar community has its own temple and also goes to other common temples also. They participate in the temple festival but they do not pay temple tax since they work and clean the surroundings of the temple.

Castes	*Social condition*	*Economic condition*	*Political condition*	*Education condition*	*Sanitation condition*
Pallar	Good	Good	Good	Good	Poor
Parayar	Fair	Fair	Poor	Fair	Poor
Arunthathiyar	Fair	Poor	Poor	Fair	Poor
Vannar	Fair	Poor	Poor	Poor	Poor

Vannar Community

There are only two households of Vannar community in this village. One household among this is that of a widow. They do not face any discrimination in accessing the public road, temple and other facilities in the village.

The major source of income for the widow is by ironing job and also widow pension.

She has knowledge about political parties. She is living in thatched house and she does not own any land and property.

Next, with regard to the other family, their major source of income is from selling milk. They do not have any other property. The household has two children and both of them are going to school.

Findings

In most of the villages Dalits are in minority with regard to population. In this village Dalits are in majority in population. We could feel discrimination to some extent from the responses of people since the caste and class systems are internalized by Indian society.

With regard to educational condition, all the children from Dalit communities are going to school and there is no dropouts. All people are spending more money for the education of their children. The economic condition of Dalits is good in this village. The Pallar community has most of the land. The Parayar community owns some land too. The Arunthathiyar and Vannar communities do not have any land.

Conclusion

In Palayankottai village Pallar community is dominant caste group and they are higher in status and power as compared to other castes. Caste discrimination is not visible yet it is being practiced. But there is invisible caste discrimination in Palayankottai village. Arunthathiyar community, even though being the second major caste group in this village lacks in all basic facilities and education as compared to Pallars.

5. Role of Traditional Local Institutions

It is practiced in Tamil Nadu villages that the traditional Panchayats perform certain responsibilities and in fact they develop conflict with Constitutional Panchayats. In many places, the traditional Panchayats play complementary role to Constitutional Panchayats. Two obvious responsibilities are being discharged by them. They are resolving small disputes among the temples. Apart from the above, there are certain other functions they perform. They vary from place to place. In this village how the traditional Panchayats play their role is being studied through this village programme.

Some individuals have been identified in the village for interaction on this subject. Many have not any inertest on this subject with an assumption that it will create unnecessary controversy. Only a section of the people evinced interest to discuss about the traditional Panchayat is Varian.

Table 5.5: Setting Disputes in the Villages

Sl. No.	Name	Traditional Panchayat Leader	Police	Court	By Themselves
1.	S. Thangavel	✓			
2.	S. Vellasamy	✓			
3.	K. Alagar	✓			
4.	V. Krishanammal				✓
5.	Murugan	✓			
6.	Mariyammal	✓			
7.	Santhanam		✓		
8.	Sadaiyan	✓			
9.	Pappathi		✓		
10.	Mariyappan	✓			
11.	Vasanthi	✓			
12.	Selvi			✓	
13.	Alaguponnu	✓			
14.	Paulraj		✓		
15.	Chinnamani	✓			
16.	Chokkan	✓			
17.	Sangeetha	✓			
18.	Ramesh	✓			
19.	Palanisamy	✓			
20.	Thangaponnu	✓			

Source: Computed.

Based on the discussions, the following points have been deduced.

(a) Each caste has its own Panchayats.
(b) It collects money from the people for temple festivals.
(c) Apart from the conduct of temple festivals, the committee resolves paltry conflict and disputes among families and individuals within their caste. It arranges marriages for the youth belonging to the same caste.
(d) It arranges marriages for the youth belonging to the same caste.
(e) The committee settles disputes between husband and wife.
(f) When there is marriage in a family the committee members are being respected.

(g) The head of the committee is much respected person.
(h) There are certain individuals and families who are not under the control of the traditional Panchayats and they went to police station.
(i) Going to court and police stations is a rare occurrence.

6. Expectation of the People from the Government

Students are interested to know the people's expectation from the governments. Governments are able to serve only on fulfilling the expectations of the people. Otherwise, in a democracy people will change the government. There are three governments, namely, Local Government, State Government and Central Government. Equally their representatives of the people are to act as link between the government and the people. How effectively the representatives are playing their role in the respective governments in aggregating the demands of the people and articulating the same in the respective authoritative bodies is to be studied from the perspective of the people. Expectations vary from segment to segment. Their expectations will be based on their aspirations and needs. Further people should know what are the responsibilities of the each tier of governance from the local government to Central Government. People should have extreme clarity on the roles of the elected representatives. In order to elicit the opinion from the people about their expectation, a study was designed and for which a brief interview schedule was prepared to conduct face to face interview.

Interview Schedule

1. Are you clear about the responsibilities of the Central Government? Yes/No
2. Are you clear about the responsibilities of the State Government? Yes/No
3. Are you clear about the responsibilities of the Local Government? Yes/No
4. Are you satisfied with the performance of the Governments? Yes/No
5. Are you casting your vote regularly? Yes/No

6. Do you think it is your responsibility to cast your vote? Yes/No
7. Are you satisfied with the performance of your MP? Yes/No
8. Are you satisfied with the performance of your MLA? Yes/No
9. Are you satisfied with the performance of Local Bodies? Yes/No
10. What do you expect from the Government?

For all the nine questions they replied negative. 49 respondents have been identified for this interaction. They are poor, marginalised, widow, aged, ordinary wage earner and poor women. Everyone said that they are not clear about the functional divisions among the three governments. Nobody came and informed us about their functioning.

When people face problems, they are to be attended to by the governments whichever is having powers, responsibilities and resources. Governments have to solve the problems of the people. They should be guarding the people and helping the people. Now people are searching for help and they write petition and searching for appropriate person to submit. They are not satisfied with the performance of the governments and performance of the representatives of the people in all the three tiers of the governance. To the question what you want from the government they replied that they need work. They are ready to work and earn their livelihood. Secondly their life expenditure has to be well within their earnings. It means price of the essential commodities to be low. Throughout their life they struggle to lead a life. It has to be changed. It should not be a struggle. All their basic needs have to be met well within their earnings. But people, however poor they are, they know one thing clear that they get help from the government and they are being treated satisfactorily by the government. They only elect the representatives. After they got elected they treat the people casually. Representatives and government have to be at the mercy of the people but now in India people are at the mercy of the government. They argued that in terms of discharging responsibilities, we are second to none. We cast our votes in the election without fail. By losing our daily wage we went to polling booth and cast our votes. Nobody can accuse the poor. Though we are uneducated and poor we are more responsible and sincere than our government and our representatives.

"We have not done any damage to the nature, we have not done anything wrong to destabilize our governance, administration. We never exploited the people. We are being exploited by all". These are the observations of the respondents. We have been seeing the people who are unethical and fraudulent they lead luxurious life. They make wealth. They make the government officials to serve them. But we are poor, harmless, sincere, obedient, rule following citizens but we are treated as secondary citizens.

Based on the observation of the respondents in the village themselves in the review meeting why is this condition for the poor in India? The students have found out an answer. It is because of the poor awareness about the functioning of the governments and their roles and responsibilities. Organisations and institutions which work with poor are divided and they are not able to organise the poor successfully. Democracy provides enormous opportunities for poor to bargain with powerful and government but these

Table 5.6: People's Knowledge on Governance

Sl. No.	*Questions*	*Yes*	*Percentage (%)*	*No*	*Percentage (%)*
1	Are you clear about the responsibilities of the Central Government?	0	0	49	100
2	Are you clear about the responsibilities of the State Government?	0	0	49	100
3	Are you clear about the responsibilities of the Local Government?	0	0	49	100
4	Are you satisfied with the performance of the Governments?	0	0	49	100
5	Are you casting your vote regularly?	49	100	0	0
6	Do you think it is your responsibility to cast your vote?	49	100	0	0
7	Are you satisfied with the performance of your MP?	0	0	49	100
8	Are you satisfied with the performance of your MLA?	0	0	49	100
9	Are you satisfied with the performance of Local Bodies?	0	0	49	100

Source: Computed.

opportunities are also exploited by a segment of the society. For many of the local needs the local body can find solution. But that local body is also weak and exploitative.

> **Box XI: People's Money, Government Discretion**
>
> There is a community hall with toilets and the toilets are not in use as there is water connection. The community hall does not have fans and tube lights. There is a community toilet which does not have water connection. Yet the women are using the toilets. Very nearer to the toilets there is a bore well which was sunk with an aim of taking drinking water. Since it has salty water, it is not in use. There is a small storage tank in the toilet complex. There is no connection between the bore well and the tank in the toilet complex. Many of the doors in the toilets are broken. When we contacted the Panchayat representatives, and asked them why these minimum facilities have not been created in the community hall and women toilet complex. They said that there is no money to do all the repair work. There is no discretion to spend the money for these repairs. At that point a lady from the same village said that from Prime Minister to Block Development Office they have discretionary fund but poor people living in the villages do not have discretionary fund. Villages are not independent. They are in the hands of the officials and Government Departments.

7. Skill Development in the Village

At present, skill development is considered as basic for economic development of the country. To sustain 8 per cent economic growth India needs 500 million skilled workforces. These five hundred million workforces are for industry alone. Available youth force can be utilized very effectively by skilling them. Series of steps have been taken to build the skill of the youth in India. In this context, students have involved themselves to find out whether marketable skills are available in the village. Apart from the above, many steps have been taken to build the skill of the youth in this village. Majority involved in agricultural activities they are manual in nature and not technology involved. Along with agriculture people maintain milch animals in every house. Majority, lead life on agriculture and animal husbandry. People who do not have land will work in agriculture as labourers. In order to find out the available skills, in the village a number of discussions were held. Based on the discussions, the students found out the following skills:

- Car Driving
- Truck Driving
- Tailoring
- Carpentry
- Masonry
- Electrical work
- Plumbing work
- Washing
- Saloon
- Fitter
- Binder
- Bike Mechanic
- Car Mechanic
- Nursing
- Inscensestick Making
- Candle Making
- Poultry Rearing

All the skills what they have are to be transmitted from generation to generation. The above skills have not been developed through proper training. They do not have any certificate. They cannot go out from the village to get jobs. Those who migrated from this village to urban areas are for mere manual labour works. Some of the participants said that in this village there is no proper guidance and counselling for the boys and girls who are in schools. Neither the parents nor the students have got clarity on education. Only a few families who have got exposure since they are travelling widely get these children educated properly and get employment. Others are always groping in dark.

Slowly people try their level best to choose appropriate course for their wards. For the people education is an instrument to fetch job and earn livelihood. Everyone says that vocational education will bring rich property to India. It is all in newspapers. How to do it? Where people can go? Nobody knows. What to do? These are the responses of some of the respondents. People in the village believe that by putting their wards in engineering college, they can earn huge amount of money. It is a myth everywhere and it is not broken. What villagers need today is proper information. Village Panchayat office should be made as information centre. Well informed individuals can help the families by providing needed information. But that is not happening in the village.

8. Students' Evaluation of Infrastructure in Schools

Students of the university who were in the camp wanted to know the perception of the children who are in public schools about the facilities available in the public schools. It was a group discussion based on the check-list prepared by the group leaders. The discussion points include the availability of teachers, infrastructure facilities in the school, meals served in the school, services rendered in the school based on the schemes of the government. For each question the students have responded well. From the answers given by the students one can easily infer that all public schools are well equipped with all basic facilities. The need of the hour is the effective utilization of all the facilities for the benefits of the students.

9. Census Data and its Validity

Since students have internet access, they have taken the print out from the census website of the Government of India about the basic statistics of the village Palayankottai. All the data available in the census website about the Panchayats have been contested by the villagers and they are being supported by some of the officials who are working in this village Panchayat. Since some basic information is needed about the village Panchayat, students have collected all those details and compiled. When they are discussed with villagers, they have concurred with the statistics. Census data and the village data compiled by students are attached herewith. There was a discussion among the students facilitated by the teachers about the need of the data base and its utility for decision-making. After an elaborate discussion students argued for data base creation at the Gram Panchayat level.

Table 5.7: Responses of the Students towards the Infrastructure Facilities

Sl. No.	Name	Are there enough teachers		Are basic facilities as black board, furniture and paraphernalia present		Mid-day meal and their menu			Government schemes			Are toilet facilities available?
		Yes	No	Yes	No	Pulses	Egg	Quality of food	Scheme that provided free books, uniform etc.	Scholar-ship for students	Computer provided under Sarva Siksha Abhiyan	
1	Karuppaiah	✓		✓		✓	✓	✓	✓	✓		✓
2	Sriraman	✓		✓		✓	✓		✓	✓		✓
3	Muniraja	–	✓	✓		✓	✓		✓	✓		✓
4	Manivasgam	✓		✓		✓	✓		✓	✓		✓
5	Pugalenthi	✓		✓		✓	✓		✓	✓		✓
6	Manokari	✓		–	✓	✓	✓	✓	✓	✓		✓
7	Meenakshi	✓	✓	✓		✓	✓	✓	✓	✓		✓
8	Jayalakshmi	✓	✓	✓		✓	✓		✓	✓		✓
9	Thamariselven	✓	✓	✓		✓	✓		✓	✓		✓
10	Aryamala	✓		✓		✓	✓		✓	✓		✓
11	Balamurugan	✓		✓		✓	✓		✓	✓		✓
12	Kausalya	✓		✓	✓	✓	✓		✓	✓		✓
13	Saravana Kumar	✓		✓		✓	✓		✓	✓		✓
14	Sriraman	✓		✓		✓	✓		✓	✓		✓
15	Kannaiya	✓		✓		✓	✓		✓	✓		✓

Source: Computed.

PRIMARY CENSUS ABSTRACT DATA (FINAL DATA)

State Name: Tamil Nadu (33)
District Name: Dindigul (612)
Sub-District Name: Attur (05765)
Village Name: Palayankottai (635430)
No. of Households: 1092

Population	*Person*	*Male*	*Female*
Total	3750	1924	1826
In the age group 0-6 years	359	199	160
Scheduled Castes (SC)	3060	1564	1496
Scheduled Tribes (ST)	0	0	0
Literate	2385	1402	983
Illiterate	1365	522	843
Total Worker	2174	1159	1015
Main Worker	2134	1142	992
Main Worker—Cultivator	87	47	40
Main Worker—Agricultural Labourers	1426	681	745
Main Worker—Household Industries	14	9	5
Main Worker—Other	607	405	202
Marginal Worker	40	17	23
Marginal Worker—Cultivator	2	0	2
Marginal Worker—Agricultural Labourers	27	9	18
Marginal Worker—Household Industries	1	1	0
Marginal Worker—Other	10	7	3
Marginal Worker (3-6 Months)	30	11	19
Marginal Worker—Cultivator (3-6 Months)	2	0	2
Marginal Worker—Cultivator (3-6 Months)	19	4	15
Marginal Worker—Agricultural Labourers (3-6 Months)	0	0	0
Marginal Worker—Household Industries (3-6 Months)	9	7	2
Marginal Worker—Other (3-6 Months)	10	6	4
Marginal Worker—Cultivator (0-3 Months)	0	0	0
Marginal Worker—Agricultural Labourers (0-3 Months)	8	5	3
Marginal Worker—Household Industries (0-3 Months)	1	1	0
Marginal Worker—Other Workers (0-3 Months)	1	0	1
Non Worker	1576	765	811

Source: 2011 Census of India, Government of India.

Household Survey (SC families)

Sl. No.	Family	Food	Dress	Toilet	Edu-cating kids	Toiletries	House type	Children	Education
1	Working as a teacher	3 times	7 pairs	Available	Private school	Monthly Rs. 50	Own tiled in *patta* land	1	Teacher training
2	Working as a clerk in BDO office	3 times	8 pairs	Available	Private school	Monthly Rs.100	Own terraced in *patta* land	2	Higher secondary
3	Working in a Mill (private) as technician	3 times	9 pairs	Available	Private school	Monthly Rs.100	Own tiled house in *porompokku* land	2	ITI
4	Working in a small factory as a technician	3 times	6 pairs	Available	Private school	Monthly Rs. 70	Own tiled house in the common land	2	ITI
5	Working in a bank as attender	3 times	5 pairs	Available	Private school	Monthly Rs. 80	Own land *pucca* house with *patta*	2	Higher secondary
6	Working in a school as a clerk	3 times	7 pairs	Available	Private school	Monthly Rs. 80	Own land RCC house with *patta*	2	Higher secondary
7	Working as bus driver	3 times	9 pairs	Available	Private school	Monthly Rs. 100	Own land RCC house with *patta*	2	Higher secondary

(*Contd.*)

(*Contd.*)

Sl. No.	*Family*	*Food*	*Dress*	*Toilet*	*Edu-cating kids*	*Toiletries*	*House type*	*Children*	*Education*
8	Working as a truck driver	3 times	5 pairs	Available	Private school	Monthly Rs. 70	*Porombokku* land, tiled house	1	10th driving skill
9	Working as technical assistant	3 times	5 pairs	Available	Private school	Monthly Rs. 60	Own house tiled with *patta*	2	ITI
10	Working as Nurse	3 times	7 pairs	Available	Private school	Monthly Rs. 70	Own land RCC house with *patta*	1	Nurse training
11	Farm worker	2 times	3 pairs	No	Public school	Nil	Hut in the *Porompokku*	3	III std
12	Road worker	2 times	4 pairs	No	Public school	Nil	Hut in the *Porompokku*	2	IV std
13	Sweeper daily wage	2 times	3 pairs	No	Public school	Nil	Land given by Govt, thatched shed	2	II std
14	Construction worker	2 times	3 pairs	No	Public school	Nil	Hut in common land	3	II std

(*Contd.*)

(Contd.)

Sl. No.	*Family*	*Food*	*Dress*	*Toilet*	*Edu-cating kids*	*Toiletries*	*House type*	*Children*	*Education*
15	Agriculture coolie	2 times	4 pairs	No	Public school	Nil	Hut in the Panchayat land	1	IV std
16	Construction worker	2 times	3 pairs	No	Public school	Nil	Thatched shed in Panchayat land	2	III std
17	Cobbler	2 times	3 pairs	No	Public school	Nil	Thatched shed in private land	3	II std
18	Agriculture farm work	2 times	3 pairs	No	Public school	Nil	Patta land given by the govt, tiled house	1	III std
19	Agriculture farm work	2 times	4 pairs	No	Public school	Nil	Patta land given by the govt, tiled house	1	II std
20	Agriculture farm work	2 times	3 pairs	No	Public school	Nil	Patta land given by the govt, tiled house	2	II std

While looking at the data provided by the households it is clear that the Scheduled Caste families who have gone for monthly work by using their educational qualification, their quality of life has been improved. In fact they all realized the value of education and importance of sanitation. In all their houses, they keep toilet and they maintain toilet culture. Even in food intake they are regular in taking three meals a day. Government has implemented plethora of schemes for the emancipation of Dalits. But all those schemes have not helped the Dalits as reservation helped the Dalits in getting admission in educational institutions and in getting jobs. Those who continued their studies and acquired some skills have got jobs by using reservation. It is unequivocal that education and reservation are two powerful instruments to transform the Dalit families.

Box XII: Data Based Questioned

In one of the review meetings some of the students have raised a fundamental question. For any decision-making particularly for rural development sector what is the exact data base? How that data are being generated? How they are validated? This question was raised in the context of the non-synchronization of the data base between NSSO and Census and other household collected for specific projects. While looking at the data base maintained by different Ministries, one will come to the conclusion that there is a problem in the data base itself. Many researchers rely on NSSO data because its reliability, as compared to other sources, is more authentic. Why students have raised this question? The reason behind this is the apparent contradiction they found between the data collected from the household and the NSSO. Then there was a discussion among themselves about the different type of data base for the same subject. For instance, Health Department of the Government projects some data which contradict the health report prepared by specialized agencies. When such a kind of confusion prevails even for the basic data base how can we expect a scientific decision-making is the question raised by some of the students. Against this background a student suggested that what is wrong in collecting base data at household level from the villages through the local bodies by evolving a suitable data generation tool. Secondly, the local governance institution can play an effective role is not only collecting data but also in validating, maintaining and updating the data. Every Gram Panchayat there is an office, officials and computer. Suitable software could be developed for data maintenance. Panchayat Secretaries and a few others could be trained in data generation and with their involvement basic data could be generated and they can be validated. This was a suggestion offered by the students after seeing the basic contradictions among the different data bases maintained for the villages.

6
Review of the Camp Activities

Everyday from the second day of the camp, review was conducted. Review of the activities carried out by the students and review of the logistics have been done. All the group leaders were asked to make a small presentation about the activities they have done in the village on the subject chosen. After the presentation students of the same group were asked to indicate the left out points. Subsequently, all the students were asked to make comments and observations. While doing so the teacher who is in the review meeting makes his/her own observation. Students used to ask questions related to theory and disconnects between the theory and practice on the issues have been explained by the teacher.

In the whole process of learning the methodological nuances adopted by the students to study the problems have been reviewed. The problems faced by them have been discussed. Students used to bring newer nuances to collect data and analyzed the same. Students interacted with wide variety of groups in the village as they are the respondents to study the problems. Along with the discussion students used to take photo video on the rural realities and brought them to review. Lot of verifications have been done after collecting relevant data. Students adopted different modes to verify the data collected from the respondents. Data collected from the Panchayat functionaries are verified with people and in the same way data collected from the parents are verified with the children of the same family.

Box XIII: Review of the Camp Activities

Review is a continuous process. It takes place in different stages. It starts from the second day of the camp. It is not a mere review of the activities carried out by the students. It has its own methodology. It is being facilitated by the teachers. It takes minimum of two to three hours. Students make presentations based on the experiences they have gained in the camp on the themes. They are being questioned by others. Based on the above a brief discussion is held. The teacher who facilitates the discussion brings in the theoretical aspects of the subjects. Just like a classroom student takes notes from the discussion. When students make presentation, it is almost a structured presentation. They are: (a) the task assigned to the group; (b) the methodology adopted for investigating the problem; (c) inferences arrived out, (d) evidences collected; (e) analysis made, (f) conclusion they make.

Since many of the students have laptops and mobile phones, the documentation process was very strong. Since students keep a group meant for photography students have used that group to take photos. While making presentations students used to bring different kinds of tools to collect data from the field. While listening to the presentation, teacher can formulate series of research problems.

Box XIV: What Improvements can be Made in the Programme?

When we (students) go to villages, we should not go in large numbers. We should go to different villages and for which we need to group of students. Seven will be the optimum number. Students should take food in the village tea stalls. We have to use the water which they use. The stay could be extended more than a week. Minimum of two weeks is necessary for the students to learn in the village. University could establish a strong link with Panchayat Institutions for continuous activities in the villages even after the Village Placement Programme. Learning needs more or less a loose structural design of the programme. This camp type programme limits the learning options. We spend more time for logistics. Some of the students' time was consumed for logistics alone. They could not give time for academic exercises.

7
Learning for the Students

On the last day we have conducted one review where the students have been asked to make a comprehensive presentation about the work they have done in the villages for the seven days. While making presentation, they have to use only Power Point Presentation with photos and videos. During the review students have informed the results of the study and explained what they have achieved and what they have learnt. Subsequently, on reaching the University at the end of the programme in the field another review was conducted after a week. In this review, students were asked to explain what they have gained in the field. The students had to explain their learning. They made the following points in the review meeting. The points explained hereunder are the points which the students made in the two review meetings:

- How to collect data from the field without giving any false promise to the respondents has been learnt through this camp.
- How to build rapport with the community has been learnt from this camp.
- Effective group learning was possible only through camps.
- How to evolve methodological nuance to collect data has been learnt through this camp.
- Tools, techniques learnt in the classrooms have been tested in the field through this camp. All the tools and techniques of PRA have been used in the field. Different kinds of focus group discussion had been conducted. Nuances of

group discussions could be learnt only through this type of camp.

- Information distance between the government and the people is noticed.
- People are in the hands of the government and government is not in the hands of the people.
- Rule of law Vs. ruling party direction has been understood through this camp.
- All institutions and organisations created in the rural areas are not with people but with government.
- Only a very few organisations are with community and they do not have legitimacy.
- Though there is sizeable population which belong to Dalits, there is no common identity with which they function. Parayar, Pallar and Arunthathiyar are the three communities who maintain their caste identity. There is no common Dalit identity.
- Programmes for poor reach only the party men and women not the really needy.
- Corruption becomes a culture and people are also part of it. It seems that per capita corruption is more than the per capita tax in the villages. Lower level corruption hits the poor in the villages.
- Government schemes are reaching the beneficiaries only through ruling party local level functionaries. The party functionaries are the development brokers.
- People do not have awareness about RTI. Nobody to help the poor to get their due from the Government schemes without paying bribe.
- Poor spent more money for temples and less for sanitation and water supply. Absolutely poor do not have any understanding of the importance of sanitation and safe drinking water supply.
- Cell phone, Televisions are with every household. When cell phone has reached every household the importance of sanitation has not reached.
- Panchayats are in the hands of the government officials and not with the people. Panchayat leaders seem to be

accountable to the government officials rather than the people.

- However, poor people have realised the power of education and that is why poor are spending more on the studies of their kids.
- Women's empowerment takes place. They articulate, connect themselves with larger society. They keep money with them. They take decision in the family.
- People has realised their duty of voting. In fact the poor only save our democracy by casting their votes without fail. Rarely do they fail to perform the obligation of casting their votes.
- Yet getting money for it is not considered as unethical as political parties are having huge corpus. As people think that political parties are making huge money, people tend to think that getting money from the party is wrong.
- People are kept away from the school, sub health centre, public distribution centre, cooperative society and they are all functioning under the control of the government. People those who are working in those institutions are not accountable to the people but they are accountable to higher officials.
- Panchayat institutions are weak in terms of their powers, finance and functionaries. Panchayat leader's capacity skill and capabilities are poor and weak. They are under the control of the officials. There is no synergy among the organisations, institutions and groups functioning at the village level. Enormous facilities have been created and huge investment has been made but utility is limited and underutilized.
- Self-Help Group (SHG) debt burden has been increased and likewise women's workload has also been increased after they become members of SHG. SHG women have come up to only credit not to the level of entrepreneurship. MGNREGA has transformed the Dalit families and more particularly the women.
- Enormous scope for research in MGNREGA.

Box XV: Knowledge and Sensitivity

While giving feedback I asked a straight question to the students, "would you feel this Village Placement Programme is useful, essential for your career?" One student V. Premalatha, II M.A. Student stood up said that it is not only useful to our career but also for our own life in the villages. She said that she is coming from a rural area but she was not sensitive on many of the issues of the people in villages. In such a way difficulties and hurdles have been internalised by the people in the villages. Only when she attended this camp she got clarity to many of the rural conditions. She further informed that she will be of much use to her family and her village as she would become a catalyst to bring transformation in the rural areas. Further she elaborated that it gives confidence to speak about the problem of rural transformation. Through books she said she gains knowledge and through field-work she gains full understanding of reality and sensitivity.

8
Feedback of a Teacher who was with the Students in the Camp in All the Seven Days

When I was student of Gandhigram Rural University I attended Nine Village Placement Programmes (VPP) during the academic years from 2001 to 2006. The VPP camp consisted of four days per semester. We used to go two times a year. I gained knowledge from the field. In 2001, I attended first camp which was an eye opener for me to understand the life and livelihood of various communities in the village. First time, I asked a respondent about their economic status. He, in turn, asked me a question that if I give details what will you do for me? At that point of time I could not understand the question. Now I could understand the question. It is a culture in our village system that whoever goes to village for data collection gives the impression that by doing the survey they are going to be helped. Only by giving false promise one can collect real data from the rural areas. Real and original data cannot be collected by giving false promises. How to come to reality and what methodology has to be adopted in the villages to get authentic and accurate data I have learnt only through this camp. I observed from the field that every community, whether they are rich or poor, expects welfare programmes from the government. The first VPP camp taught me the following concepts: communication, group dynamics, community behaviour, values and ethics in the villages. Remaining eight camps, I attended in different villages for VPP. Before going to the camp I and my friends used to prepare a plan to make the camp more meaningful in the villages. After entering into village, our (me and my friends) plan has been changed to suit the requirements. The tasks of the camp had been given to us and we divided ourselves into many groups. I was either a member of a group or I was a group leader. If I was a member I had limited responsibility, if I was a leader I have lot of responsibilities. During these camps, I gained practical knowledge from the field. The first practical knowledge was the application of 73rd Amendment to the Constitution of India. Our teachers taught us the 73rd Constitution Amendment Act in theory but not explained in practice. Consequently, I gained practical knowledge in the field about the functioning of the New Panchayati Raj system. I gained knowledge about group dynamics, leadership, transformation, institutions and organisations only when I came to the field and worked with people.

After joining as a teacher of this Department, Prof. G. Palanithurai has given me an opportunity to attend this VPP camp as camp in charge. First time as a teacher I came to the village along with the students. My mandatory function is to act as facilitator and stay with the students in all seven days. I have attended first VPP came with students and research scholars. Before going to camp, Prof. G. Palanithurai has given some ideas about camp and gave me liberty. I have responsibility to indicate the capabilities coming out from the students when they are at work. Therefore, sixteen committees have been created and responsibilities have been assigned. A committee consists of five members and a leader. They have to study the activities of Panchayat, expectation from the Government, Panchayat and MLA/MP, livelihood condition of the poor, opportunities for entrepreneurship, corruption in governance, infrastructure of the Village Panchayat, voting responsibility of voters, conflict management, conditions of sanitation, social relationship, problems of single family and poor family, conditions of *Dalits*, health conditions of women and children and skills available.

Freedom has been given to students and tasks of the camp have been completed within the stipulated time. Everyone enthusiastically participated. It is observed that above 90 per cent of the students have actively involved all the process of the camp. The programme schedule has been made by students and they regularly followed it meticulously. I did not ask students to do programme. They actively participated in all activities of the camp. As a teacher what I observed from the camp is that students have a tendency to learn more about the issues only from the field and not from the classrooms. They exhibited their creativity only through field-work. When they are in action one could notice their innate ability, skill, capacity, leadership and so on. In the classroom setting one could see only one set of the skills not the other. Their learning ability is enhanced only through the camps. Their concern for the community, poor, marginalized and their passion could be seen only from the field.

Methodology

Students have adopted an array of methods and used series of tools for collecting data about the aspects they are interested in studying in the Village Placement Programme (VPP). Mostly they followed one to one interaction, focus group discussion, Participatory Rural Appraisal methods, verification visits, formal meetings, informal indirect conversations with respondents. Methods and tools have been decided by the students depending on the nature of the topic. Senior students and mostly final year students have guided others. Since they are preparing for dissertation, they have undergone two courses in Research Methodology and Statistics. They were able to guide the junior students.

9
Learning for the Teachers

Primarily the teachers could see the enthusiasm of the students in learning mode. Teaching development theory and studies in classrooms is more a mechanical process rather than an organic exercise. When the students are in the field it becomes development practice. Students can bring in more clarity to concepts, frameworks, approaches and theories only in the field. While sailing along with the students in development practice teachers can generate volley of problems to be investigated. If the teacher is a committed researcher, he or she can generate intricate researchable problems from this type of camps.

All the above problems could be investigated properly by the Department with the help of the Research scholars and master students. Since, the students have allotted hours for extensions in a week, that time can be used for collecting data for the project. Teachers when they teach in the classroom, they found many riddles in the transformative process of the rural communities. All those riddles can be investigated through field visits and extension.

It is found out that students have used variety of tools and techniques to collect data for analysis. The tools used by the students are raw and unrefined. They can be further sharpened and they can be used. Many innovative tools will be generated by the students when they are in the field. The students have to be facilitated.

Village needs an enabler or a catalyst to coordinate and synergize the institutions and organizations and by doing so village transformation could be positive, effective and development oriented. At present there is no synergetic activities.

When teachers and students visit villages, people from the villages come to them to seek some information from the teachers and students.

Sl. No.	*Villagers' Problems*	*Directions*
1.	A few farmers sought the help to get information input	We have directed them to meet the training official of KVK
2.	A few parents sought the help to get information related to academic problems	We have advised them to contact a few Departments in the university
3.	A few demanded information related to toilet construction	We directed them to contact the sanitation department
4.	Panchayat leaders want some information relating Panchayat administration	From Rajiv Gandhi Chair for Panchayati Raj Administrative Manual was provided
5.	For SHG members training is needed on some skills	We directed them to approach Gandhigram Trust which will conduct the training programme
6.	For the unemployed graduates who prepare for Bank examination need some support	We directed them to approach Ayakudi free coaching centre for this purpose

From this Village Placement Programme as a coordinator what I found out are many and of which data base creation at the grassroots is the basic. I have developed it as a theme for a National seminar jointly with Institute of Rural Management, Anand, Gujarat.

10
Conclusion

Based on their stay in Palayamkottai Gram Panchayat, Aathoor Block Panchayat and their study on different aspects of the transformative process of the village communities a few conclusions are drawn. They are:

- In a village Gram Panchayat works, Village Administrative Office works, public distribution shop works, cooperative society works, traditional Panchayat works, party functionaries work, sub-health centre works, school works. Self-Help Group works, a large number of retired government employees are living and yet they never met each other for the development of the village and they never develop a vision for the development of their village. Unless a plan is evolved with the active participation of the villagers, there will not be any synergy among the people's organizations and institutions.
- People have never felt that they are being helped and facilitated by the government. They feel that their life is entirely based on the activities of the Government. Why this negative feeling towards the government? It is realized that people should feel that it is their government and it is working for them. To cultivate such a feeling government machinery has to treat people as their masters. They exist only for them. But now it is other way round. The bureaucracy should create a feeling among the people that they are the servants of the people. The existing human

relationship between the people and the government is no way different from colonial administration. People those who are registered as member of political party which is ruling the state or the Central Government feel that they are the government and they will make and unmake things. In the villages they decide things and they dictate terms to Panchayats and other officials at the grassroots level. To get any benefit from government one has to get the support of the ruling party functionary.

- Enormous amount of information are needed to people to lead a decent dignified human life. They need basic information about sanitation, water, health, personal hygiene, nutrition, skill, education, employment, savings, government schemes, government departments, and so on. If any educational institution helps the communities by providing more information needed to them on a sustainable basis, communities and rustic folks will be transformed. Their life conditions will be changed. At present information are available but not to the required level and required form. People need information useable at their end. Such a way packaged information are needed.
- In India, for decision-making and policy-making we need reliable database. But all our data generation starts from district level. But today in our country one will find contradiction Census Data and NSSO data, NSSO data and human development data. All activities are carried out at the ground. No break up data available down below the block level. On any development issue one can easily contest the position of the government by showing the data generated for specific purpose. As institution for governance is available at the grassroots, data generation can be initiated from Gram Panchayat level. To generate data from the village Panchayat data generating tool has been prepared by the Planning Commission and the plan plus software developed by the Ministry of Panchayati Raj can be effectively used for this purpose. It is not only for data generation but also for micro plan preparation at village Panchayat level. It is the normal question raised by people

about the plan. When we prepare a plan, where do we go for resources for implementation of the planned activities? We need not seek money from elsewhere. We try our level best to match the needs with the schemes of both the governments. For the gap villagers can approach the MP and MLAs for resources from the constituency development fund.

- In India, the higher learning institutions have not discharged all the three essential functions. Research, teaching and outreach activities are the three core functions and they are to be done professionally by the higher learning institutions. But in reality our higher learning institutions have performed the two functions namely teaching and research and not the outreach function. This is the major gap we identify through our extension activities throughout. There is no serious and systematic thinking at the policy level for integrating extension activities in the curriculum of higher learning institutions. To make it to happen it is necessary to develop a discourse on this theme. From our experience in the village stay for a week and work with people we found a lot of activities can be done by the academic activities for the benefits of the community and the students. Our big question is—

Why our policy community does not think seriously about integrating extension into our curriculum of higher learning system?

PHOTO GALLERY

Inauguration by BDOs

2. Review of the Activities

3. Students in the Field

4. Students in Awareness Creation

5. Students in Prayer

6. Students in Shramdaan

7. Student's Interactions

8. Students Meeting in the School

9. Students in Presentation

10. Students in PRA Activities

11. Student's Cultural Activities

12. Students' Group Discussion

13. Student's Social Map activities

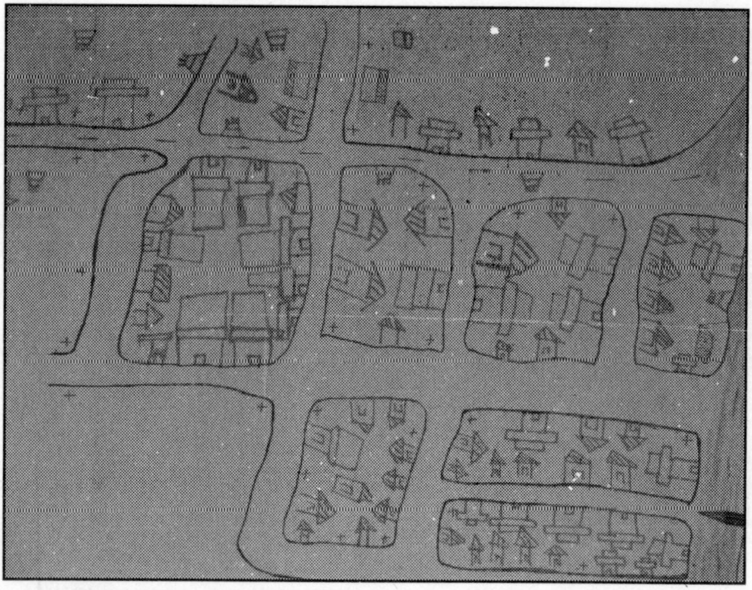

Index